Messiaen: *Quatuor pour la fin du Temps*

Anthony Pople

University of Southampton

PUBLISHED BY THE PRESS SYNDICATE OF THE UNIVERSITY OF CAMBRIDGE
The Pitt Building, Trumpington Street, Cambridge CB2 1RP, United Kingdom

CAMBRIDGE UNIVERSITY PRESS
The Edinburgh Building, Cambridge CB2 2RU, United Kingdom
40 West 20th Street, New York, NY 10011–4211, USA
10 Stamford Road, Oakleigh, Melbourne 3166, Australia

First published 1998

Printed in the United Kingdom at the University Press, Cambridge

Typeset in Monotype Ehrhardt 10.5/13pt

A catalogue record for this book is available from the British Library

Library of Congress cataloguing in publication data applied for

ISBN 0 521 58497 3 hardback
ISBN 0 521 58538 4 paperback

AP

for Flora

Contents

Contents

Acknowledgements

A number of people have helped me towards the writing of this book, notably Henrietta Brougham and Hilary Thomson at United Music Publishers and Père Jean-Rodolphe Kars in Paris. I should also acknowledge the lively contributions of dozens of students in my seminars on this work at the Universities of Lancaster and Southampton.

I owe a special debt to Peter Hill, who invited me some years ago to produce what became a much admired series of his recorded performances of Messiaen's works for piano. Working in minute detail on this music was an education for me that finds partial fruition in this small volume. I should also like to thank Peter for his comments on a draft of the book, together with Ian Hare. Ian Darbyshire, with whom I have had numerous illuminating conversations on Messiaen over the past few years, kindly allowed me to see in typescript his essay 'Messiaen and the Representation of the Theological Illusion of Time'.

Christopher Dingle, who is writing a biography of Messiaen, also read the book in draft and commented on it in depth. Besides correcting a number of errors, he generously suggested improvements and provided helpful materials. Julian Rushton as ever was a source of wisdom and good advice at the same stage. Needless to say, no-one but myself is responsible for any shortcomings that remain. Others whose willingness to help at critical moments eased my task included Jeanice Brooks, Siglind Bruhn, Philippa Bunting, Lisa Whistlecroft and the staff of the National Sound Archive. The staff of Cambridge University Press have been unfailingly encouraging and helpful to me, above all Penny Souster.

Amidst considerable domestic disruption, Angela, Lucy and Flora contrived somehow to give me the space I needed to write the book. My previous contribution to this series was dedicated to Lucy; this book is dedicated to Flora, who is not yet old enough to know. I trust that when the time comes she will take the dedication as it is meant: a token of loving hope and faith in her future.

Music examples from the *Quatuor pour la fin du Temps* are reproduced by permission of Editions Durand S. A., Paris/United Music Publishers, Ltd. To them I am also grateful for permission to present passages from Messiaen's preface to the score in my own translation. Music examples from Messiaen's *Technique de mon langage musical* and *Les corps glorieux* are reproduced by permission of Editions A. Leduc, Paris/United Music Publishers Ltd.

Introduction

In May and June 1940 the German Chancellor Adolf Hitler conducted a remarkable campaign of war which culminated in an Armistice treaty signed with the French government of Marshal Pétain in a railway carriage north-east of Paris on 22 June. The military thrust which led to this notorious but pragmatic political settlement had begun at dawn on 10 May with an invasion of the Netherlands and Belgium. By the end of the month both countries had fallen; British troops had fled to the coast in their thousands and were being evacuated from Dunkirk by a vast flotilla of boats large and small. At the same time, several hundred miles to the east, many French troops were taken prisoner as the German armies moved relentlessly onward from the Belgian border.

One of these was the young composer and organist Olivier Messiaen. He was thirty-one years of age, round-faced and bespectacled, and was serving in a menial capacity for the medical corps. Messiaen and three companions were captured in a forest by German troops as they reached the end of a journey by foot from Verdun to Nancy.[1] Together with countless others he was held in an open-air camp pending transit from the war zone to the heart of Hitler's empire,[2] and after a long and arduous journey by rail arrived at a prisoner-of-war camp known as Stalag VIIIA, at Görlitz, a small town in Silesia about 55 miles east of Dresden.

In captivity, Messiaen was stripped of his uniform but managed somehow to retain a haversack containing a small and eclectic collection of pocket scores – from Bach's Brandenburg Concertos to the *Lyric Suite* by Alban Berg. This library, he said later, 'was to be my solace at a time when I would suffer, as the Germans themselves suffered, from hunger and cold'.[3]

1

Messiaen's early career

At the time of his capture Messiaen already had several major works behind him. Born in 1908 to artistic parents and precociously talented, he had entered the Paris Conservatoire at the age of 11 and had won first prizes there in counterpoint (1926), piano accompaniment (1927), organ (1929) and composition (1930). Devoutly religious, he had been appointed organist at l'Église de la Trinité in Paris in 1931 – a conventional office curiously at odds with his radical musical sensibilities.

Even before leaving the Conservatoire, Messiaen had composed two works of great imagination and distinction – *Le banquet céleste* for organ (1928) and the eight Preludes for piano (1928–9) – and others, notably the orchestral work *Les offrandes oubliées* (1930) and *L'Ascension* (for orchestra, 1932–3; rewritten for organ, 1933–4) would soon follow. These works are recognised today (though hardly at the time) as remarkably mature in their absorption of a wide range of influences, some of them exotic. Paris in the 1920s was a giant melting-pot of cultures, and whilst in music that decade has come to be dominated in hindsight by the works of Stravinsky and the composers of the group 'Les six', there was in fact a vast range of other strands in Parisian musical life, on some of which Messiaen seems likely to have drawn.[4]

First, there are the influences Messiaen himself acknowledged, such as his composition teacher Paul Dukas (1865–1935). Dukas allowed few of his works to survive, and the popularity of *L'Apprenti sorcier* does not necessarily show him to posterity in his best light. Far more impressive and influential, both on Messiaen and on others – such as those Viennese musicians, including Berg for example, who saw it produced there in 1908 – was his opera *Ariane et Barbe-bleue*.[5] This work shares with Debussy's *Pelléas et Mélisande* its origin in a play by the Belgian symbolist Maurice Maeterlinck, but it is more inscrutable than Debussy's work and its tone is altogether darker. Messiaen knew *Pelléas* perhaps even more thoroughly than *Ariane*, as its score had been a tenth-birthday gift from his boyhood harmony teacher Jehan de Gibon (whom we should thank also):

> A provincial teacher had placed a veritable bomb in the hands of a mere child. ... For me, that score was a revelation, love at first sight; I sang it, I played it, and sang it again and again. That was probably the most decisive influence I've received ...[6]

Messiaen would later recall that as a student at the Conservatoire he was the only one who possessed the scores of Schoenberg's *Pierrot lunaire* and Stravinsky's *The Rite of Spring*. But these modernist talismans were not at the centre of his musical world: 'I was closer to Debussy. I remained loyal to my childhood loves: Debussy, Mozart, Berlioz, Wagner.'[7] Messiaen's love of Debussy's music and his admiration for Dukas as man and artist meant that despite his appreciation of Honegger and Milhaud,[8] the origins of his style lay firmly with the generation of French musicians that preceded 'Les six' rather than with the post-war innovations of that group.

Among other influences that Messiaen was to acknowledge from his teachers the most far-reaching was that of Marcel Dupré and Maurice Emmanuel, who between them introduced him to ancient Greek rhythms and trained him in their musical application.[9] Dupré (1886–1971) was both Messiaen's organ teacher and his link with the great French organ tradition exemplified in the 1920s also by Widor and Tournemire. He used improvisation on Greek rhythms as a pedagogical tool and wrote about them in his *Traité d'improvisation*, which was published in 1926 while Messiaen was still a pupil at the Conservatoire. Emmanuel (1862–1938) was Messiaen's music history teacher, though he regarded himself primarily as a composer. His course on Greek metre, though of a year's duration, merely whetted Messiaen's appetite, encouraging him to visit libraries in search of further information from which he developed his own understanding of the subject. In Messiaen's own words:

> Greek metres rely on a simple and essential principle: they are composed of shorts and longs; the shorts are all equal and a long equals two shorts. ... Metre is quite simply the grouping of two feet, the foot being a rhythm composed of a certain number of short and long values each having a precise name.[10]

He goes on to explain how one foot may be substituted for another – not necessarily of the same overall length – and how the total of the note-values in a verse is thus not infrequently a prime number. These observations underpin what Messiaen terms his 'secret predilection for prime numbers (5, 7, 11, etc.)' in his preface to the score of the *Quatuor*.[11]

Translated from poetry to the domain of musical rhythm, this view of metre as a consequence of the interplay of long and short values may be seen as a foundation of something highly characteristic of Messiaen's style from the mid-1930s onwards. Instead of the even beats and bars which are the traditional basis of Western musical metre, Messiaen worked, in effect, with beats of irregular length: not, for example, regular crotchets, but groups that are three, four or five semiquavers in length, all juxtaposed in apparent freedom.[12] There is still an underlying regular pulse, but it is at the level of this tiny 'short' value rather than that of the slower perceptible beat, which is delightfully uneven.

Messiaen's study of Greek metre was not the only catalyst for this stylistic development, for he had also made a study of classical Indian rhythms through a chance encounter with the *Saṅgītaratnākara* ('The Ocean of Music'), a thirteenth-century treatise authored by Śārṅgadeva.[13] Although the *Saṅgītaratnākara* is only one of many ancient Indian sources on Saṅgīta – the art of song, instrumental music and dance[14] – it was on this treatise that he alighted and from which he learned of the deçi-tâlas ('regional rhythms'). These were rhythmic formulæ not dissimilar to the Greek 'feet' in their combination of short and long values to produce effects quite alien to the Western classical tradition, and which Messiaen clearly found both fascinating and musically invigorating. He used the deçi-tâlas in his own compositions and also took from a study of the *Saṅgītaratnākara* the principle of 'non-retrogradable rhythm':

> Whether one reads from right to left or from left to right, the order of their values is the same. This peculiarity is found in all rhythms divisible into two groups each of which is the retrograde of the other, with a 'shared' central value.
>
> For example … A succession of non-retrogradable rhythms (each bar contains one such rhythm):

> This is used in the sixth movement of the *Quatuor*: 'Danse de la fureur, pour les sept trompettes'[15]

The synthesis of Indian and Greek elements that developed in Messiaen's mind is shown by his keen identification of a non-retrogradable long–short–long pattern in rhythms typical of the dance music of Crete.[16] To this mix should be added his devout appreciation that the neumes of plainsong were similarly liberated from the bars and beats of Western music.[17] Messiaen's understanding of this wealth of ancient precedent allowed him to acknowledge Stravinsky's use of additive rhythm, most famously in *The Rite of Spring*, without being beholden to Stravinsky as a source of his own style.[18]

It was nonetheless through the Franco-Russian cultural axis that Messiaen – who 'didn't approve' of the musical æsthetics inspired among a generation of French composers by Jean Cocteau's *Le coq et l'arlequin* (1918) and *Le rappel à l'ordre* (1926)[19] – may have come to be influenced by a group of musicians younger than Debussy and Dukas. Links between Russian and French music from the latter part of the nineteenth century onwards were legion, including Debussy's formative contacts in Russia with Tchaikovsky's patron Nadezhda von Meck and her family in the early 1880s, and the seminal visits of Sergei Diaghilev's company to Paris that began with a series of concerts in 1907 and developed into the *Ballets Russes* – giving the world such works as *The Firebird*, *Petrushka*, *Daphnis et Chloë*, *Jeux* and *The Rite of Spring*. Messiaen's own enthusiasm both for Musorgsky's *Boris Godunov* and for Russian folksong is well recorded.[20] Martin Cooper has compared Dukas's work, and *Ariane et Barbe-bleue* in particular, with the style of Rimsky-Korsakov,[21] but Messiaen's connection with Rimsky comes about more by virtue of the fact that both men associated the senses of sight and sound through synæsthesia – seeing colours when they heard music. A more recent Russian composer who shared this capacity was Alexander Scriabin (1872–1915), who in a series of grandiose and ultimately apocalyptic projects had presented his own creative force as an expression of the divine, inspired initially by the theosophical writings of Helena Blavatsky.

The detailed spiritual content of Scriabin's work must have been repugnant to Messiaen, which may explain why his only public acknowledgement of Scriabin's existence is in connection with synæsthesia.[22] But the points of technical contact between Scriabin's late style and elements of Messiaen's 'musical language' are highly evident (see chapter 2); and, as Paul Griffiths has noted, a number of younger Russian composers strongly influenced by Scriabin were among the émigrés working in Paris in the 1920s in the aftermath of the 1917 revolution and the civil war that closely followed it. One of these was Ivan Vishnegradsky (1893–1979), whose habitual use of quarter-tones in his mature music was certainly known to Messiaen.[23] Another was Nikolai Obukhov (1892–1954), whose works were considerably more bizarre in their spiritual dimension even than Scriabin's own, frequently relishing as if masochistically the physical details of quasi-Christian martyrdom. It is difficult to believe that Messiaen knew any of this music closely; but he will surely have been aware of the presence and activities of these composers and of other musicians associated with Scriabinism, such as the gifted musical commentator Boris de Schloezer.[24] And whatever his misgivings about their specific beliefs, he would also not have failed to notice their conviction that music had a spiritual dimension – something which set them in significant contrast to the group of 'Les six' and all it stood for.

By the mid-1930s Messiaen was himself preparing to join forces with other French composers in a named group with its own manifesto. This was 'La jeune France', which gave its inaugural concert in June 1936. Its members, other than Messiaen, were André Jolivet (1905–74) – the most prominent in the group at its formation – and two lesser-known composers, Daniel Lesur and Yves Baudrier. Their stated intention was to present 'a living music, having the impetus of sincerity, generosity and artistic conscientiousness',[25] but as Antoine Goléa points out, only Jolivet and Messiaen were intent on achieving this through new musical means.[26] This grouping of four men, always disparate, was made irrelevant by the war, but Messiaen evidently retained his admiration for Jolivet's piano work *Mana* (1935), which in its exotically magical subject matter seems to anticipate some of Messiaen's post-war music.[27]

Messiaen's pursuit of the spiritual through an innovative musical language drawing on many sources continued in the mid- and late 1930s. The four major works of these years stand close to the *Quatuor* in style, and were likewise cited liberally by the composer in *Technique de mon langage musical*, a two-volume treatise written on his repatriation to France and published in 1944, in which he set out the main elements of his rhythmic, melodic and harmonic techniques, together with his approach to musical phrasing and form, and much else be-sides.[28] The prefaces to the published scores of both the *Quatuor* and the organ work *La Nativité du Seigneur* (1935) introduce important concepts that were to be discussed at fuller length in *Technique*. Whereas the preface to the *Quatuor* deals in the main with matters of rhythm, including non-retrogradable rhythms and the 'added value' (*valeur ajoutée*) – an isolated 'short' beat, in the terminology of Mes-siaen's Greek metrics – the preface to *La Nativité* gives the first intro-duction to Messiaen's most notable conceptual innovation in the sphere of musical pitch: the 'modes of limited transposition' (see Ap-pendix). Messiaen developed the idea of modal composition from his familiarity with the church modes, from the music of Maurice Em-manuel,[29] and probably also from the Russians.[30] His own most fa-voured modes are highly characteristic in their melodic and harmonic implications, and feature prominently in the other major works of this period: the song cycle *Poèmes pour Mi* (voice and piano, 1936; voice and orchestra, 1937), the *Chants de terre et de ciel* (voice and piano, 1938) and the organ work *Les corps glorieux*, which was completed in August 1939, just prior to the full outbreak of war and only a matter of months before its composer's capture and incarceration.

Genesis of the *Quatuor*

Messiaen was grateful that his German captors regarded him as harm-less and left him more or less alone. Not only was he allowed to retain his collection of scores, but an officer gave him music paper, pencils and erasers.[31] There was no piano yet to be had, but this did not stop him composing. With him in Stalag VIIIA were three other musicians, including his superior from the medical corps, the cellist Étienne Pasquier. The others were a clarinettist, Henri Akoka, who had been with them in the transit camp near Nancy,[32] and a violinist, Jean le Boulaire. In Messiaen's own words:

> I immediately wrote for them an unpretentious little trio, which they played to me in the lavatories, for the clarinettist had kept his instru-ment with him and someone had given the cellist a cello with three strings. Emboldened by these first sounds, I retained this little piece

under the name of 'Intermède' ('interlude') and gradually added to it the seven pieces which surround it, thus taking to eight the total number of movements in my *Quatuor pour la fin du Temps*.[33]

The 'Intermède' is indeed an unpretentious piece which presupposes little or no familiarity on the part of its performers with the complexities of Messiaen's 'musical language'. Yet some of the other movements in the finished *Quatuor* embody his technical innovations just as rigorously as the *Chants de terre et de ciel* and *Les corps glorieux* had done. It would seem that Messiaen needed to coach his players thoroughly – Pasquier recalled how the German officers would listen respectfully as they rehearsed together every evening at 6 o'clock[34] – and one may readily surmise that the 'Advice to performers' at the end of the composer's preface to the score is a souvenir of this work:

> In the non-metric pieces such as 'Danse de la fureur ...', they may count the semiquavers mentally to help themselves, but only in the earliest stages of rehearsal; doing this in a public performance would make it tiresomely dull: they should keep the feeling of these values, nothing more.
>
> ... they should not be afraid of the exaggerated nuances – the accelerandos, rallentandos, all that makes an interpretation lively and sensitive. The middle of 'Abîme des oiseaux', in particular, should be full of fantasy. Sustain implacably the extremely slow speeds of the two eulogies [*louanges*], to the eternity of Jesus and to His immortality.[35]

The requirements of this practical work, through which the players gained familiarity with Messiaen's style over a period of time, would seem likely to have been reflected in the order in which the movements were composed. In addition, the numerous cross-references between the movements give clues as to the likely order of their composition after the 'Intermède'. But the situation is rendered more complex by Pasquier's recollection that the movement for solo clarinet that became the third movement of the *Quatuor* was actually written in the transit camp, i.e. before Messiaen had even reached Stalag VIIIA:

> It was in this camp that Akoka sight-read the piece for the first time. I was the 'music stand', which is to say that I held the score for him. He grumbled from time to time, as he found the composer had given him difficult things to do. 'I'll never manage it', he would say. 'Yes, yes, you'll see', answered Messiaen.[36]

Though at first sight incompatible with the composer's version of events, these memories seem too vivid to be dismissed. If the two accounts are to be reconciled, one must surely conclude that the music which Akoka sight-read in a field simply formed the basis for a more developed piece that Messiaen finalised in Stalag VIIIA at a later date. This would in fact strengthen the comparison to be made between the third movement and the other two 'solo' movements – the fifth and eighth – both of which were transcribed from pre-existing works by Messiaen after he had resolved to compose the *Quatuor* as a multi-movement work in which his instrumental forces would be varyingly deployed.

Indeed, the full ensemble of four instruments is used only in the first, second, sixth and seventh movements. Of these, the sixth stands apart in that the instruments play in unison or octaves throughout: the movement could easily have been rehearsed by Messiaen without a piano, and is perhaps ideally written for this purpose. Its rhythms are for the most part firmly in Messiaen's ametrical style, and indeed give a textbook illustration of the 'added value', but there are moments where the music seems to step back momentarily into something more regular, only to launch itself anew into Messiaen's language. All of this, together with the fact that its main theme is taken directly from the 'Intermède', suggest that it was the next of the movements to be composed.

By comparison, the third movement in its final form is rhythmically freer than the sixth, not only in general but also in its treatment of some specific musical materials shared between the two. The solo clarinet writing incorporates imitations of birdsong into its melodic palette, though in a way that by Messiaen's later standards is rudimentary: the calls of individual birds are not differentiated and the birdsong passages are comparatively brief. Nonetheless, Messiaen chose to cite the first such passage from this movement at the very outset of his discussion of birdsong in *Technique*, and one may reasonably speculate that this reflected his memory of the order in which the birdsong passages in the *Quatuor* were composed.

The second and seventh movements are closely related to each other in musical material and, insofar as the seventh movement is in many ways a development of the second, there can be little doubt that they were composed in the order in which they appear in the finished work. The second movement develops the birdsong materials from the third, whilst in the violin and cello parts it retains to a considerable extent the octave unison textures of the sixth. The seventh movement gives complete independence to the instruments, and – if this supposed order of composition is correct – would have been the first of which rehearsal was next to impossible without a piano. Messiaen's remark that 'I did not have a piano [when I began to put the work together], and I didn't hear what I had written until much later'[37] is not at odds with this interpretation of events, since so much of the material of the seventh movement is taken from the second – which might indeed have been written, and sections of it brought to rehearsal, before Messiaen had an instrument to hand.

As mentioned above, the fifth and eighth movements were transcribed, presumably from memory, from two of Messiaen's earlier compositions. In the *Quatuor*, each is scored for solo string instrument with piano accompaniment. The eighth movement is taken from the second part of the organ work *Diptyque* (1930); its melody is cast in a fairly conventional 4/4 metre and could easily have been practised by the violinist, le Boulaire, without accompaniment. The same may be said – although it is less regular in metre – of the fifth movement. This was rewritten for cello and piano from a section of *Fête des belles eaux*, a work which Messiaen had composed in 1937 for an ensemble of six *ondes Martenots*.

Because these movements share no material with the rest of the *Quatuor*, it is difficult to speculate with confidence about the stage at which they were transcribed for incorporation into it. Whilst in terms of rehearsal requirements they are comparable with the movement for solo clarinet – and it is probably no coincidence that the sixth, third, fifth and eighth movements are those referred to by Messiaen in his 'Advice to performers' – they are more akin to the first movement with regard to their place in the work's overall layout.

Taken together, these three movements – the first, the fifth and the eighth – frame the *Quatuor*, and each is concerned with the contemplation of eternity:

> This *Quatuor* comprises eight movements. Why? Seven is the perfect number, the six days of Creation, sanctified by the Divine Sabbath; the

seven of this rest is prolonged into eternity and becomes the eight of everlasting light, of eternal peace.[38]

We cannot hope to tell, however, whether Messiaen planned the overall shape of the *Quatuor* at an early stage or whether it emerged only as the movements were accumulated – though he must surely have had a clear vision of the work when deciding to relate the second and seventh movements so closely. If the transcribed movements were prepared after this, there would still be no reason to think that Messiaen's decision to re-use music he had already composed was dictated by shortage of time, as one might suppose of a work composed under normal conditions of musical life. He may, however, have judged the style of these movements to be more suited to the strengths of their performers than something written in his newest idiom would likely have been.

Be that as it may, it seems highly probable that the first movement, 'Liturgie de cristal', was the last music to be composed specifically for the *Quatuor*. Its use of birdsong is the most differentiated of all the movements in which such material appears; and its use of Messiaen's most complex rhythmic devices demands a great deal of its performers if accuracy is to be maintained, whilst also giving leeway for errors of co-ordination to arise without unduly spoiling the overall effect.

Theological inspiration

Although chamber music was rare in Messiaen's output, the *Quatuor* is close to the centre of gravity of his work in its union of theological inspiration and technical achievement:

> Its musical language is essentially immaterial, spiritual and Catholic. Modes which achieve a kind of tonal ubiquity, melodically and harmonically, here draw the listener towards eternity in space or the infinite. Special rhythms, beyond metre, contribute powerfully in dismissing the temporal.[39]

This combination of straightforward technical description with mystical Catholicism is typical of Messiaen, and can seem disconcerting. But to see these two aspects of his thought as paradoxical is to read him in the context of Romantic notions of the Artist. On the contrary,

11

Messiaen's calling was more that of the medieval religious craftsman: seeking technical perfection in the tangible phenomena of nature, he adopted no less factual a tone when writing about theological matters. The details of the afterlife were as real to him as the harmonic series and the 'mysteries' of prime numbers, and his works deal with all these things on an equal footing.

The score of the *Quatuor* is inscribed: 'in homage to the Angel of the Apocalypse, who raises a hand towards Heaven saying: "There shall be time no longer"'. The Biblical reference is to chapter 10 of the book of Revelation, which he quotes selectively in his preface to the score, omitting the passages shown here in italics:

1 And I saw another mighty angel come down from heaven, clothed with a cloud: and a rainbow was upon his head, and his face was as it were the sun, and his feet as pillars of fire:

2 *And he had in his hand a little book open:* and he set his right foot upon the sea, and his left foot on the earth,

3 *And cried with a loud voice, as when a lion roareth: and when he had cried, seven thunders uttered their voices.*

4 *And when the seven thunders had uttered their voices, I was about to write: and I heard a voice from heaven saying unto me, Seal up those things which the seven thunders uttered, and write them not.*

5 And the angel which I saw stand upon the sea and upon the earth lifted up his hand to heaven,

6 And sware by him that liveth for ever and ever, *who created heaven, and the things that therein are, and the earth, and the things that therein are, and the sea, and the things which are therein,* that there should be time no longer:

7 But in the days of the voice of the seventh angel, when he shall begin to sound, the mystery of God should be finished, *as he hath declared to his servants the prophets.*[40]

This text, as he told Antoine Goléa, was simply a starting point: 'I did not want in any way to make a commentary on the book of Revelation, but only to justify my desire for the cessation of time.'[41] Nonetheless, a commentary was part of the work's original presentation, since its performance in the camp was preceded by a lecture given by Messiaen himself on the book of Revelation:[42]

I told them first of all that this quartet was written for the end of time, not as a play on words about the time of captivity, but for the ending of concepts of past and future: that is, for the beginning of eternity, and that in this I relied on the magnificent text of the Revelation ...[43]

No further details of Messiaen's commentary can be ascertained, but a passage he wrote for Goléa's book gives some idea of his views on the subject, albeit nearly two decades later:

With regard to the apocalyptic character [of the *Quatuor*], to regard the Revelation merely as an accumulation of cataclysms and catastrophes is to understand it poorly; the Revelation also contains great and marvellous lights [*lumières*],[44] followed by solemn silences. Moreover, my initial thought was of the abolition of time itself, something infinitely mysterious and incomprehensible to most of the philosophers of time, from Plato to Bergson ...[45]

Messiaen was convinced that musicians were as well placed to investigate the nature of time as were scientists or philosophers, saying that 'Without musicians, time would be much less understood.' He saw his use of non-retrogradable rhythms and other devices as somehow operating on time itself, revealing its nature.[46]

At least one concept found in Messiaen's commentary on 'the end of time' that demands closer consideration is 'the beginning of eternity'. Iain Matheson compares theological conceptions of eternity with Plato's attempt 'to express the unity of past–present–future':

'was' and 'will be' are created species of time which we in our carelessness mistakenly apply to eternal being. For we say that it was, is and will be; but in truth 'is' applies to it, while 'was' and 'will be' are properly said of becoming in time.[47]

According to this view, eternity does not – cannot – 'begin', because it simply 'is', whereas the Christian theological conception, which Messiaen shared, requires time both to begin and – at the apocalypse – to be brought to an end. If this seems to present a logical difficulty, then it is a difficulty which is also found, as Ian Darbyshire has noted, in Messiaen's ontology of rhythm in cosmological terms:

Suppose that there were a single beat in all the universe. One beat; with eternity before it and eternity after it. A before and an after. That is the birth of time. Imagine then, almost immediately, a second beat. Since any beat is prolonged in the silence that follows it, the second beat will be longer than the first. Another number, another duration. That is the birth of Rhythm.[48]

Darbyshire identifies in this account 'a confusion of ideas ... caused by the distinction Messiaen makes between Time and Rhythm':

> The thing which comes before and after in relation to Messiaen's single beat is eternity, but eternity by definition exists outside of time and so cannot be numbered as an antecedent or consequent of change in relation to that single beat. Relation between time and eternity, and relation between points in time, are not equivalent relations.[49]

As if to expose these underlying issues to view, Messiaen's *Quatuor* contains on the one hand movements that contemplate qualities of eternity, and on the other hand movements that are concerned with the events of the apocalypse as described in the book of Revelation. The work's most palpable evocation of 'endlessness' is to be found in the opening movement, perhaps suggesting that this form of eternity is fundamental; in contrast, after the seventh and most cataclysmic movement comes a 'eulogy [*louange*] to the immortality of Jesus', evoking through Christian interpretation the eternal life which comes only when time itself is brought to an end.

First performance

Messiaen's *Quatuor pour la fin du Temps* was not the only musical work of consequence to be produced in captivity, even during the same war. Perhaps the most dreadful story of this kind is that of the Czech composers Pavel Haas, Hans Krása and Viktor Ullmann, whose incarceration in the concentration camp town of Terezin (Theresienstadt) was merely a staging post on their journey to the gas chambers, along with countless others, in 1944. Their musical achievement in these utterly desperate conditions more than bears comparison with Messiaen's as a victory through art of humanity over inhumanity. But Messiaen's focus of attention was significantly different from that of the Terezin composers, just as his imprisonment was not the same as theirs in nature. Whereas they knew for certain that they were living on borrowed time – which surely motivated Ullmann's use of heavy satire in the opera *Der Kaiser von Atlantis* ('The Emperor of Atlantis') – Messiaen was driven to contemplate time in a quite different way, focusing on theological truths about the end of *all* time in contrast to the uncertain end of his incarceration. The musical result – the *Quatuor pour la fin du Temps* – went along with a feeling of detachment from his physical circumstances:

> If I composed this quartet, it was to escape from the snow, from the war, from captivity, and from myself. The greatest benefit that I drew from it was that in the midst of thirty thousand prisoners, I was the only man who was not one.[50]

It was in line with this extraordinary detachment that Messiaen later denied that the title of the *Quatuor* was a play on words about the end of time in captivity. All he would admit to was a punning desire for the end of musical time, in the sense that he wished in this work above all to eliminate the regular beats of classical music.[51] It is just possible to believe that Messiaen's unswerving faith allowed him to focus exclusively on the theological import of his music, even at the first performance. But one can be fairly sure that many of his fellow prisoners, listening to a work about the day of judgement, would have allowed their thoughts to alight on their future deliverance, and on their captors being brought to account before the Almighty.

The first performance must indeed have been an awesome and unforgettable occasion:

> After [my] lecture, they brought in an upright piano, very out of tune, and whose key action only worked intermittently.[52] It was on this piano, with my three fellow musicians, dressed very strangely, myself clothed in the bottle-green uniform of a Czech soldier, badly torn, and wearing wooden clogs ... that I was to play my *Quatuor pour la fin du Temps*, in front of an audience of five thousand, among which were gathered all the different classes of society: peasants, labourers, intellectuals, career soldiers, medics, priests ...[53]

Also among them was a Polish architect, Aleksander Łyczewski, whose acquaintance with the *Quatuor* was movingly and unexpectedly to be renewed after forty years when in the autumn of 1981 he and his wife took as a lodger in Warsaw the British authority on Polish music,

Charles Bodman Rae, who – without knowing Łyczewski's wartime background – was at the time preparing for a performance of the *Quatuor*:

> One day, I heard Aleksander Łyczewski rushing downstairs from his painting studio and he then burst into my room with a mixed expression of confusion and distress on his face. He said he recognised the piece I was playing and wanted to know who had composed it. He sat down and I explained about Messiaen and the circumstances under which the *Quatuor* had been written and first performed. He then recounted to me his experience as a prisoner of war in the same camp at Görlitz in Silesia. Aleksander was in a very emotional state while he was recalling these events. There were tears in his eyes and it took some time for him to regain his composure. He had been present at the first performance and vividly recalled the atmosphere in the large freezing hut where hundreds of prisoners (many Poles, other central Europeans, and some French) assembled to hear the piece. Apparently there were even wounded prisoners, brought from the hospital block, lying on stretchers at the front of the audience. He remembers his fellow-prisoners remaining in complete silence for the hour or so that it took to perform the piece. He himself had been deeply moved by the experience.[54]

Rae generously wrote to Messiaen to tell him of this, and the two former inmates of Stalag VIIIA began an intermittent correspondence that continued until the composer's death in 1992.

Łyczewski's experience of the first performance must have been shared by many who were in that audience on 15 January 1941. Nearly twenty years afterwards, Messiaen was to recall with humility that he had 'never … been listened to with such consideration and understanding'.[55]

1

Liturgie de cristal

Between three and four in the morning, the awakening of birds: a solo
blackbird or nightingale improvises, surrounded by a shimmer of
sound, by a halo of trills lost very high in the trees. Transpose this onto
a religious plane and you have the harmonious silence of Heaven.[1]

Messiaen's description of the opening movement presents a conjunction of Heaven and the natural world that was to become central to the
expression of his musical theology. This movement, 'Liturgie de cristal', shows us as it were in embryo something that would come into
larger existence with *Des canyons aux étoiles ...* and *Saint François
d'Assise*. But it is an embryo that is already fully formed, not least
because its anatomy is on one level quite straightforward.

Interpretations

Messiaen's audacity lies in the very simplicity of his means, but these
are employed in the service of the profound. In 'Liturgie de cristal',
fragmentary imitations of birdsong, played by the clarinet and violin,
are heard alongside unchanging and continuous material played by the
cello and piano. It is easy enough to arrive at a provisional interpretation of these musical facts: clearly, one might say, the two latter instruments in some way represent Heaven; and given the work's title we
might assume our focus is on Heaven's eternity. Indeed, as we shall
see, the music of the cello and piano is constructed so that in concept it
is perpetual – without beginning or end. The birds, we might conclude, are held in this musical frame like prehistoric insects preserved
in amber, caught on the wing; though such birds would not be historical creatures, for they would exist outside our world of past, present
and future.

Ex. 1.1 *i*/A:1–4, clarinet[2]

The distance that opens up between Messiaen's music and even such an immediate interpretation as this one is a space inhabited by difficult questions of representation and signification. In considering these, it is perhaps useful at the outset to distinguish between the symbolic and the literal, if only to see how this distinction is undermined by Messiaen's approach. The clarinet's opening music, for example, imitates the song of the blackbird (Ex. 1.1).[3] Its freedom from the musical constraints of barlines and easily assimilable tonal organisation makes it likely to be heard not so much as a melody that merely suggests birdsong, however, but more as a literal attempt to transcribe elements of the blackbird's characteristic song within the limitations of the instrument chosen. What we hear 'is' a bird; and a second bird – the nightingale – is heard when the violin begins. Yet, in the terms of our initial interpretation of the music, Messiaen's purpose would appear to be symbolic: firstly since these birds can be no more than a mere pair of representatives of the company of Heaven, and secondly because we know that we are not hearing a literal transcription of the sound of Heaven itself. Indeed, Messiaen's programme note speaks of Heaven's 'harmonious silence' – a condition his music cannot hope to attain but merely to represent. Something of the obverse would thus apply to the music of the piano and cello, since what they play cannot signify Heaven other than symbolically. Nonetheless, their music 'is' without beginning or end – the same patterns cycled and recycled with no apparent articulation in time. At the very least, it is as if, each time we listen to the *Quatuor*, for these three minutes or so we are eavesdropping on something everlasting.

Through their musical conjunction, this quality attaches itself to the birdsongs also, and herein lies a significant distinction between Messiaen's prose description and the music of 'Liturgie de cristal'. The words outline events that happen in space and time – specifically, between three and four in the morning – whereas the music has little or no narrative quality. Indeed it cannot, for the presentation of the 'endless' music of the piano and cello requires such articulation to be withheld. Messiaen's words moreover invite us to 'transpose' these temporal events 'onto a religious plane' – something which, being an act of interpretation, also happens in time. It is not quite clear whether Messiaen expects us to hear the movement in its entirety as a depiction of the dawn chorus, transposing it Heavenwards in our minds only on reflection, or whether we are to accomplish this reflection as we listen. But in either case the interpretation is far richer than was the plausible first impression outlined above – of birds held in an unending tableau – since we are forced to find a place for the 'Heavenly' music of the cello and piano in our temporal world. In terms of the scene Messiaen describes in his note, the endlessly repeating sounds stand for the 'shimmer', for something present in the stillness of the morning – for the 'halo' lost in the trees.[4] But if music is 'lost', then surely it merges with silence? And if so, we are indeed thereby put in touch with the 'harmonious silence' of Heaven. This comes about only as a result of shuttling back and forth in our minds between the earthly and the Heavenly – between the temporal and the 'end of time' – and the way in which we are obliged to hear the musical scene in these two ways simultaneously serves to drain the distinction between the symbolic and the literal of its interpretative power.[5]

But this last point is entirely in line with Messiaen's faith, in which the Communion bread 'is' the body of Christ, and the wine His blood. This movement's 'liturgy' of cut-glass, of crystal, simply *identifies* the silent halo of God's presence at each new dawn with the silent harmonies of Heaven. And there can indeed be no doubt, from all the evidence of his life, that Messiaen's faith was absolute – as if the agnosticism of the humanist renaissance, and all its consequences for the interpretation of how the temporal relates to the spiritual, had simply never happened. Yet his musical technique – of which he was justly proud – allowed others to be party to his conception.

Technique

In terms of musical organisation, the greatest rigour is to be found in the material played by the cello and piano. To take the cello part first: its material is simply a fifteen-note melody (Ex. 1.2) which is repeated continuously throughout. As the melody repeats, the positions of its notes in relation to the barlines change, but the note-values remain the same. (The additional tied quaver beat across the barline at bars *i*/F:2–3,[6] which slightly disrupts this scheme, seems likely to have arisen as an oversight.) The close of the movement interrupts the cello about midway through its eighth repetition.

This melody exemplifies a number of aspects of Messiaen's technique. The first concerns its pitches: only C, E, D, F♯ and B♭ are heard, all of which lie within the same whole-tone scale (from which only A♭ is missing). The whole-tone scale, considered simply as a collection of pitch-classes (pcs),[7] is one of a small number of such collections that have a particular property much prized by Messiaen. This is the property of 'limited transposition'. Transposing these six pcs up by one semitone yields a different whole-tone collection (D♭, E♭, F, G, A, B);[8] but a further transposition brings us back immediately to where we began. The whole-tone scale is in fact the first of seven 'modes of limited transposition' that Messiaen outlined in his writings (see Appendix). Of all of them, it is the one he used most sparingly – apparently because he felt its potential had been exhausted by earlier composers such as his teacher, Dukas.[9] But Messiaen uses it here nonetheless. Comparison with other instances of mode 1 in his works suggests that it may have been acceptable to him in this instance because the pitches are not as readily perceptible when played in the form of artificial harmonics on the cello as they might be if presented differently, and because other harmonic systems are simultaneously in operation, so that the overall texture is far from being straightforwardly whole-tone.

A second observation that can be made about the pitches of the cello part is that the sequence C–E–D–F♯–B♭ itself repeats three times within the fifteen-note melody,[10] and thus twenty-one times (nearly twenty-two!) in all. This fact is to a small extent obscured by the different rhythmic presentations of its three occurrences in the melody

Ex. 1.2 *i*/A:2–8, cello (sounding pitch)

(♩♩. ♩♩♪ / ♪♩. ♪♪♪ / ♪♩. ♪♪♩).[11] Indeed, the conceptual separation of the pitches and rhythms in the cello part is an altogether remarkable feature.

Considering the rhythm in isolation – just as we have previously been considering the pitches in isolation – the fifteen-note sequence exemplifies another of Messiaen's most characteristic innovations, one to set alongside the modes of limited transposition. This is the principle of 'non-retrogradable rhythm': a rhythm which because it is a palindrome, i.e. the same backwards as forwards, cannot be presented in retrograde (a simple example might be ♩ ♪ ♩ – or, counting in quavers: 2 1 2). It is easier to see this principle in operation in the melody of Ex. 1.2 if one divides it into two groups – 4 3 4 quavers and then 4 1 1 3 1 1 1 3 1 1 4 – each of which is palindromic.[12] Alternatively, one may realign the sequence, which is after all 'endlessly' repeating, so that it begins with the sixth note-value from the end, thus – 1 1 3 1 1 4 4 3 4 4 1 1 3 1 1 – to make a single non-retrogradable sequence of fifteen values.[13]

Turning to the piano part, we may observe that it too repeats a rhythmic sequence, this time made up of seventeen note-values (♪ ♪ ♪ ♪♪♪ | ♪♪♪ ♪ ♪ ♪♪ | ♪♪ ♪ ♪). This rhythm seems to have been a personal favourite of Messiaen's: he had already used it in the *Chants de terre et de ciel* and *Les corps glorieux*, and would later make striking use of it in the *Visions de l'Amen* (1943).[14] The derivation of its first six note-values from the retrograde of the rhythmic formula *râgavardhana*, taken from the *Saṅgītaratnākara*, is outlined at the very outset of *Technique de mon langage musical*;[15] the next seven present the formula *candrakalâ* and the last four *laksmîça*.[16] Unlike the cello's

Ex. 1.3 'Harmonic pedal' in piano part

sequence this is not a non-retrogradable rhythm: it simply repeats over and over.

Like the cello, however, the piano has a repeating pitch sequence, namely the cycle of twenty-nine chords shown in Ex. 1.3. The first two of these chords present a characteristic harmonic progression, founded on what Messiaen calls the 'chord on the dominant'. According to his discussion of this in *Technique*, the pitch-class collection from which the chord is derived is not one of the modes of limited transposition, but the traditional diatonic (major) scale. To begin with, this is set out vertically on the fifth degree of the scale (the dominant) in the form of a chord amenable to tonal usage (Ex. 1.4a). Its function as a dominant ninth chord emerges, according to Messiaen, when three of the notes are resolved as appoggiaturas within the scale (Ex. 1.4b). Messiaen's individual development of this sonority comes by taking the two upper appoggiaturas, and their downward resolution in parallel through a whole tone, as a model. Moving back a stage, as it

Ex. 1.4 Derivation of 'chord on the dominant'

were, he applies this double appoggiatura configuration to the original seven-note chord, producing an initial sonority which lies outside the diatonic collection and yet resolves into it (Ex. 1.4c).[17]

Messiaen freely adapts this progression of two chords by rearranging the notes so that the lowest is not necessarily the fifth degree of the underlying diatonic scale. This is what happens in chords 3–4, 5–6 and 7–8 of the piano's sequence. But if there is some confusion in the fact that the so-called 'chord on the dominant' may not actually be supported by the dominant note itself,[18] there is an important aspect of consistency in Messiaen's retention of an F♮ in the bass throughout the passage, even as the underlying diatonic collection shifts from B♭ major to A♭ major, F major and C major. This use of a pivot note in the bass was a matter of considerable significance to the composer because of its synæsthetic quality. Frequently in his writings he associates it with a play of colour: at this point in *Technique de mon langage musical* he describes it as the 'effect of a stained-glass window' and gives a second demonstration of it with a different type of chord.[19]

The continuation of the piano's chord sequence is less tightly structured, but Messiaen ensures there are connections from one chord to the next, and generally also across larger spans. Chords 9–12, for example, retain the bass F from the opening 'stained-glass' pattern. In the middle register of each of these chords is a first-inversion major triad, and these triads rise chromatically from one chord to the next: G♭ major in chord 9, then G major, A♭ major and A major. The uppermost line initially retains the E from the top of chord 8; this note also continues in chord 10, at which point the G below is doubled at the higher octave, 'reaching over' – to use a Schenkerian term[20] – to create a new upper voice. The high G is then retained in chords 11 and 12, at which point another new upper voice is placed above it, not this time emerging from the middle register of the same chord, but instead anticipating enharmonically the topmost note of chord 13.

The remaining chords divide into three groups according to the mode from which their pitches are drawn. Chords 13–15 lie within the diatonic collection of G♭ major, though none is strongly reminiscent of a tonally functional chord in that key. On the contrary, it is a plain G♭ major triad in the left hand of chord 16 that links it back to this group of diatonic chords, but here the right hand simultaneously plays a B♭ major triad. This combination of triads at a distance of four semitones (ic4)[21] initiates a group of six chords lying within a single transposition of Messiaen's third mode, of which this is a generating interval (see Appendix).

The last eight chords lie within Messiaen's mode 2, though not in all cases at the same level of transposition (chords 22–28 are within t1, chords 21 and 29 within t2). Mode 2 has received considerably more attention, both from composers and from writers on music, than Messiaen's other modes. Widely used by Stravinsky and others, it has come to be known as the 'octatonic' collection (or scale), and is remarkable for the quantity of triads, dominant sevenths and other tonalistic chords that can be extracted from it.[22] Something of this can be seen in the piano's chord sequence at this point. The lowest four voices of chords 23–27 descend stepwise through the mode in a manner that is thoroughly typical of Messiaen's early music: in this pattern, chords 24 and 26 have the sonority of dominant thirteenths, and these alternate with major triads, each in second inversion with added augmented fourth (e.g. chord 23: F–B♭–D plus E♮).[23] The latter chord-type is simply transposed twice more to give chords 28 and 29.

In the language of Messiaen's *Technique*, the unvarying repetition of the rhythms in the cello and piano parts makes each function as a 'rhythmic pedal' – defined as 'An independent rhythm which constantly repeats itself, without paying heed to the rhythms which surround it' – whilst the cello's repeating pitch sequence is similarly termed a 'melodic pedal' and the piano's long chord sequence a 'harmonic pedal'.[24] This terminology alludes to the so-called 'pedal notes' that in many works by J. S. Bach, for example, are sustained in the bass underneath changing harmonies (the word 'pedal' recalls how the notes were played on Bach's instrument, the organ). Messiaen's expansion of the term to apply to rhythms, melodic lines and chord progressions has far-reaching consequences. Although a Bachian pedal-note may be sustained for several bars, it is, in concept, a single note extended: its resolution with the texture above it typically comes at a single identifiable instant – often the attack-point of the final tonic harmony of the piece – at which point the conceptual origin of the pedal-note is to be found. Messiaen's rhythmic, melodic and harmonic pedals cannot exist without the passage of musical time, but they use it in a different way. The time occupied by the fifteen notes of the cello's sequence, for example, is analogous to the single instant that is the origin of a Bachian pedal. Strictly speaking, the attack-point of a musical pitch does not vanish like a Euclidian point in space (since it has to have a minimum length in order for the vibrations of a musical pitch to exist at all). Nonetheless, we may say that Messiaen's equation of a melody, rhythm or chord progression in each case with something notionally instantaneous transforms musical time so that its normal, articulated time-spans – with their beginnings, middles and ends – are conceived as but moments. Conversely, his expansion of a single point in musical time into something tangible invokes the infinite.

In 'Liturgie de cristal', Messiaen conjures this illusion in part by ensuring that the moment of resolution of the piano's rhythmic and harmonic pedals with the cello's sequence is never heard – indeed, never even comes into prospect. He does this by making use of prime numbers vastly to elongate the cyclic processes in the cello and piano. The fact that the cello's sequence of five pitches repeats exactly three times within its rhythmic pattern is the exception here: in contrast, the piano's 17-note rhythm and 29-chord sequence do not mesh neatly at all; nor do the overall patterns of the piano and the cello mesh neatly with one another. The *indivisibility* of prime numbers – which is what underlies this failure of the patterns to interlock except on a vast scale – is, along with the 'non'-retrogradable rhythms and the modes of 'limited' transposition, a further example of what Messiaen termed the 'charm of impossibilities', which he explained as follows:

> It is a glistening music we seek, giving to the aural sense voluptuously refined pleasures. At the same time, this music should be able to express some noble sentiments (and especially the most noble of all, ... the truths of our Catholic faith). This charm, at once voluptuous and contemplative, resides particularly in certain mathematical impossibilities [in] the modal and rhythmic domains. Modes which cannot be transposed beyond a certain number of transpositions, because one always falls again into the same notes; rhythms which cannot be used in retrograde, because in such a case one finds the same order of values again ... Immediately one notices the analogy of these two impossibilities and how they complement one another, the rhythms realizing in the horizontal direction ... what the modes realize in the vertical ...[25]

Looking briefly at the full extent of the cycles Messiaen has set up in this movement, we see that successive entries of the cello's 33-quaver rhythm begin at the 8th quaver of the piano's first rhythmic statement, then at the 15th quaver of the next statement and at the 22nd, 3rd, 10th, etc. of subsequent statements. It would, then, return to the 8th quaver after thirty-three complete statements of the piano's rhythm – which is to say, well beyond the end of the movement. More than this, however: twenty-nine complete statements of the piano's rhythmic material are required in order for the piano itself to bring its rhythm and its chord-sequence back to their original alignment. The numbers 29 and 33 are prime to each other (i.e. they have no common factor), so that 29×33 complete piano rhythms would be required to bring the music of both cello and piano together back to the same point, which at Messiaen's metronome mark would take approximately 230 minutes.[26]

Messiaen writes of birds that 'their songs ... make extremely refined jumbles of rhythmic pedals'.[27] This observation tallies with the music of the violin and clarinet in 'Liturgie de cristal', which is composed not of fragments which literally repeat, as does the music of the cello and piano, but of fragments which are heard many times in lightly varied forms, as if in improvisation. For example, the music of the violin is based throughout on variants of the five patterns shown in

Ex. 1.5

(a) Fragments from violin part

(b) *i*/G:1–2, clarinet (modes 1, 2 and 3)

Ex. 1.5a. The clarinet's music proceeds similarly, on the basis of the material shown in Ex. 1.1, and its continuation.

The composer was candid about the impossibility of transcribing birdsong precisely, however, and indeed we find throughout his works that Messiaen's birds sing their song with something of his own accent:

> Personally, I'm very proud of the exactitude of my work; perhaps I'm wrong, because even people who really know the birds might not recognize them in my music, yet I assure you that everything is real; but, obviously, I'm the one who hears, and involuntarily I inject my reproductions of the songs with something of my manner and method of listening.[28]

This can be seen distinctly in the clarinet part of 'Liturgie de cristal' at bars *i*/G:1–2, where the rising flourish of the 'bird' ascends through concatenated forms of Messiaen's modes 1, 2 and 3 (Ex. 1.5b). Nonetheless, the other-worldy quality of this movement owes as much to the birdsongs as to its fantastically revolving cycles – and in particular to the way in which 'their melodic contours, those of [the blackbird] especially, surpass the human imagination in fantasy'.[29]

2

Vocalise, pour l'Ange qui annonce la fin du Temps

The first and third sections (very short) evoke the power of the mighty Angel, crowned with a rainbow and clothed by a cloud, who sets one foot upon the sea and one foot upon the earth. In the middle section – these are the impalpable harmonies of heaven. On the piano, gentle cascades of blue-orange chords, garlanding with their distant carillon the quasi-plainsong chanting of the violin and cello.[1]

A *vocalise* – Rachmaninov's for soprano and piano (1912) is a famous example – is essentially a song without words. It is not an instrumental composition, however, as are Mendelssohn's *Lieder ohne Worte*, but a wordless song *for a singer*.[2] So, as in the case of the contact between nature and Heaven effected in 'Liturgie de cristal', Messiaen's use of the term *vocalise* here seeks to perform an act of identification. The song in this second movement 'is' a song for the Angel, though what we hear are the instruments of the *Quatuor*.

Form

As Messiaen's prefatory remarks explain, the movement falls into three main sections. This large-scale articulation, which immediately distinguishes the 'Vocalise ...' from the manner of the first movement, is made crystal clear by the tempo markings in the score.

The first part begins in the *modéré* tempo ($\quarternote$ = c. 54) of the previous movement, but is here additionally marked *robuste* in reflection of the musical character; after two bars comes a virtual doubling of the notated tempo (*presque vif, joyeux*, $\quarternote$ = c. 104), and these two tempi continue to alternate, ending with the *presque vif* at ii/C:1–2 and the *modéré* at C:3–7. The second section is completely different in mood and tempo (*presque lent, impalpable, lointain*, $\eighthnote$ = c. 50), and extends from D:1 to the bar before H. Finally, the third section (H:1–7) is a varied restatement of the music of C:1–7.

Ternary form, then, is the basic outline; but the organisation of the individual sections and the relationships between them add greatly to the interest of this scheme. Firstly, we may note that the reprise of *ii*/C:1–7 takes place in an almost literal inversion: rushing upward scales in the violin and cello at C:1–2 are matched by rushing downward scales at H:1–2 (the notes are in each case those of mode 3). In C:3–5, an A major triad, decorated by trills, is built and sustained through successive entries of the violin, cello and clarinet, playing the top, bottom and middle notes respectively; this is matched at H:3–5 by a D major triad which accumulates in the inverted order bottom–top–middle.[3] The third bar in each case features a flourish in the piano, combining major triads of C and G♭ before landing on an exposed major ninth: it rises upwards at C:5, descends at H:5. The more deliberate, crashing piano figures at C:6 and H:6 reverse these directions of motion, but remain otherwise in correspondence with each other (they are discussed in further detail below). Finally at C:7 and H:7 an accented chord on the piano accompanies a mordent-like figure in the clarinet – regaining in each case the tonality of the trilled triad sustained just previously.

Secondly, there is an important link between the *presque vif* material in the opening section and the principal melody in the *presque lent* middle section. The latter is undoubtedly the *vocalise* of the title: in his description of the movement Messiaen terms it a *mélopée* – a kind of chanted recitation of poetry or scripture – and likens it to plainsong (the opening bars are shown in Ex. 2.1a). Speaking many years later, Messiaen made a number of remarks about plainsong that cast an interesting light on this melody and its treatment in the *Quatuor*:

> Only plainsong possesses at once the purity, the joy and the lightness necessary to send the soul towards Truth. Unfortunately ... plainsong is poorly understood. ... And the first offence of our immediate predecessors was its harmonisation. It was written in an age when the encumbrance of chords ... was unknown. One must sing it without any accompaniment. It should also be sung by all voices: by men, women and children. Finally, it should be sung with appreciation of and respect for the neumes. ...

Ex. 2.1

(a) *ii*/D:1–3, cello (doubled by violin two octaves higher)

(b) *ii*/B:1–3, cello (doubled by violin two octaves higher)

Neumes are melodic formulæ, analogous to those that harmony texts call embellishments, appoggiaturas, passing notes – but on a much larger scale. They are also found in the songs of birds: the garden warbler, the blackcap, the song thrush, the skylark and the robin sing neumes. And what is admirable about the neume is the rhythmic suppleness it engenders. ...

Let us add that this refinement in plainsong can only manifest itself in swiftness and joy.[4]

The melody of the central section in this 'Vocalise ...' undoubtedly possesses rhythmic suppleness, and an examination of its finer detail reveals a number of recurring patterns that could be conceived as neumes. It is perhaps initially surprising, then, given Messiaen's remarks about his unnamed 'immediate predecessors', to find that he accompanies the melody so fully in the piano – though this can scarcely be described as a harmonisation. Also, the tempo is extremely slow by normal standards, quite in contrast to what Messiaen says about 'swiftness and joy'. On the other hand, the melody's presentation by violin and cello two octaves apart may be taken to suggest a combination of voices such as he advocates for plainsong. Remarkably enough, this same instrumental layout is also used in the first section of the movement, at *ii*/B:1–3, to present the identical sequence of pitches, but shorn of their neumatic rhythm (Ex. 2.1b).[5] The marking at this point – *presque vif, joyeux* – fulfils in anticipation, as it were, the composer's demand for the swiftness and joy that will reveal the power

Ex. 2.2 (a) *ii*/A:2, clarinet; (b) basis in 'chord on the dominant'

of plainsong to lift the spirit. It is as if only the two passages taken together manifest both the power and the essence of plainsong: Messiaen separates these aspects in order to create a musical form, as he describes in his prefatory note. And indeed, hearing this movement after 'Liturgie de cristal', we may readily accept the articulation of form as something less definitively temporal than it might be in other circumstances: as we listen, it is not and need not be clear which of these two 'quasi-plainsong' passages is the model, or which the transformation.

Some aspects of the opening section remain to be described in greater musical detail. The clarinet's material uses three items familiar from 'Liturgie de cristal': melodic formulæ from both the blackbird's song (*ii*/B:2–4 and B:7–8, from *i*/A:1–2, etc.; see Ex. 1.1, p. 18) and that of the nightingale, which was played in the previous movement by the violin (*ii*/B:4–5 and B:8–9; see Ex. 1.5a, p. 27). The opening of the clarinet part in 'Vocalise ...' (Ex. 2.2a) arpeggiates the 'chord on the dominant' with double appoggiatura (discussed on pp. 22–3). The chordal version of this figure that underlies the clarinet's bravura flourish is shown in Ex. 2.2b.[6]

The 'chord on the dominant' also features considerably in the piano part. The spectacular crashing descent at *ii*/C:6 extracts chords 1, 3, 5 and 7 from the piano's sequence in 'Liturgie de cristal' (see Ex. 1.3, p. 22), each transposed downward through ic4: it thus presents four successive forms of the 'chord on the dominant' with double appoggiatura, but omits the corresponding chords of resolution. The pitch-class in the bass remains constant throughout – whether spelled as C♯ or D♭ – but the entire figure descends through four octaves. (The first of these chords may be compared with the underlying basis of the clarinet flourish in A:2 and B:6, Ex. 2.2b.) In the reprise at H:6, the same sequence of chords is presented, now transposed downwards so

Ex. 2.3 *ii*/B:6, piano

that the bass of all four is B♭; the direction of their motion is inverted like the rest of the reprise, however, so that the figure is now an ascending one.

At *ii*/B:6–7, the piano has a resonant figure based intriguingly on two forms of the 'chord on the dominant' that are linked in a particular way. The music as it appears in the score is shown in Ex. 2.3: the A♯ and E♯ at the top of the first chord are the appoggiaturas which resolve to G♯ and D♯, at which point the seven sounding notes comprise the 4♯ (four-sharp) diatonic collection of E major. The two bass notes that almost immediately enter *sfff* perhaps sound indistinct in pitch in such a low register, but their pitches have been chosen by Messiaen with care: now, the seven lowest sounding notes comprise the 2♯ diatonic collection, and the G♯ and D♯ stand as unresolved appoggiaturas (their potential notes of resolution, F♯ and C♯, are of course already sounding). A transposed version of the same constellation of chords is heard at the next *modéré* (B:8–9). Note that the initial chord in this instance is again rooted on C♯, though it is based on a different diatonic collection (6♯). In fact, these two chords are taken, though in retrograde, from the crashing descending figure at C:6.

Working back towards the beginning of the 'Vocalise ...', then, we might expect to find the other two chords from *ii*/C:6 in the resonating sonorities of bars B:5–6 and A:1–B:4. Indeed, one may find traces here of those two chords – and we have seen how the opening clarinet flourish is based on one of them directly – but the music of the opening gestures in the piano defies straightforward explanation. Messiaen's own account of the opening bar of the movement describes the

32

bass dyad (C, B♭) as an example of 'inferior resonance' – a term which, though it seems to have no scientific basis in acoustics, is evidently conceived as a counterpart to the resonances of the upper partials that accompany every sounding note.[7] One might imagine that Messiaen means to imply that a bass note of this kind transforms what lies above it into its own upper (or 'superior') resonances, though this is by no means clear from the examples he gives.

A more tangible configuration is something Messiaen specifically calls the 'chord of resonance', which is based on his detailed perceptions of the upper partials of an acoustic note:

> If I play very loudly a low C on the piano, after a few seconds I will hear, successively and very distinctly layered, the first sounds that are called the 'natural resonance of sounding objects'. If I possess a normal ear, I will hear another C, higher than the first (at the octave), then a G (the fifth). If I have a sharp ear I hear beyond that an E (the third); finally, a very musical ear hears B♭ and D (the seventh and the ninth). Personally, I hear additionally an F♯ (augmented fourth), quite strongly, and an A♭ (minor sixth), very weak. Then come a multitude of higher harmonics, inaudible to the unaided ear, but of which we may get some idea when we hear the complex resonance of a tamtam or a great cathedral bell.[8]

The notes Messiaen mentions by name, together with the next audible note in the sequence of harmonics (B♮) are arranged vertically thus:

to form his 'chord of resonance'.[9] This chord is intimately connected with mode 3, in that it lacks only one note from that mode, in the form: D–(E♭)–E♮–F♯–G–A♭–B♭–B♮–C (cf. Ex. 2.1). In the 'Vocalise ...', the resonant sonority at the end of bar *ii*/A:1 (Ex. 2.4a) indeed has a C in the bass and contains six of the notes of this mode – though among them, it must be said, is the E♭ (D♯) which belongs only in the mode and not in the 'chord of resonance' on C. Although the vertical arrangement of the notes here is also quite different to that of the textbook 'chord of resonance', this is not inconsistent with the phenomenon of the upper notes' being transformed into resonances at the entry of the bass dyad.

Ex. 2.4 (a) *ii*/A:1, piano; (b) *ii*/B:5, piano

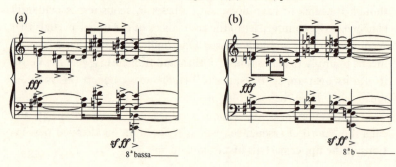

A variant of this opening music is heard at *ii*/B:5ff., with the first sounds – an example of Messiaen's comparatively rare mode 4 – transposed downward by a whole tone (Ex. 2.4b). The resonant sonority here (third crotchet beat) is again underpinned by a bass dyad covering a minor seventh (E, D), thus referring back to the chord of inferior resonance at A:1. But there is also a forward connection to the way in which the 'chord on the dominant' is treated in the next bar: in effect this minor-seventh dyad substitutes for the perfect fourth (A, D) which, if it were to occur by analogy with that next phrase, would similarly turn the entire sonority into a 'chord on the dominant' with double appoggiatura. However, this would entail the double appoggiatura – the self-same A and D – standing at the bottom of the chord, rather than in the usual place near the top of the texture.[10] Suffice it to say that what emerges from all this is that the second phrase acts as a complex transition from the first to the third, binding together the harmonic trajectory of this section of the movement despite its vivid array of flamboyant and heterogeneous gestures.

Colour

Deeply personal associations between the perception of colour and sound were important to many of Messiaen's works, perhaps none more so than this one, of which he later wrote: 'During my captivity, it was *coloured dreams* [des *rêves colorés*] that gave birth to the chords and rhythms of my *Quatuor pour la fin du temps*.'[11] The most direct evidence of the composer's concern with colour in the music is to be found in his description of the piano music at the opening of the second section as 'gentle cascades of blue-orange chords ... [a] distant carillon'. The example of 'Liturgie de cristal' perhaps suggests that the function of the piano is to play the music of something ethereal – which is seen or felt but not heard – so that the quasi-plainsong *vocalise* is understood to be accompanied by an aura, rather than inappropriately by a harmonisation, just as the presentation of its notes at *ii*/B:1–3 and B:6–7 is accompanied merely by resonance. (Messiaen's word 'carillon' alerts us to effects of resonance here as well.)

Diverse composers have associated sound with colour, sometimes in quite specific ways that affected their work directly: Rimsky-Korsakov and Scriabin are perhaps the best-known examples, while Messiaen himself cites the Lithuanian composer Mikolajus Ciurlionis.[12] In Scriabin's case, as with Messiaen by his own account, the synæsthetic phenomenon seems to have been connected with acoustical resonance.[13] The best documented instance of Scriabin making compositional use of his colour-hearing was in the notation for *tastiera per luce* ('keyboard of light') in his tone poem *Prometheus: The Poem of Fire* (1908–10), the musical substance of which was based on a pc collection similar in concept to Messiaen's modes (though not in this case of limited transposition). According to Scriabin's sometime associate Leonid Sabaneev, this 'mystic chord' was derived from the upper partials of its harmonic root.[14] The similarity in principle with Messiaen's 'chord of resonance' is striking, but Scriabin's 'mystic chord' has fewer notes and is a little different in organisation (C–F♯–B♭–E–A–D): it unaccountably omits the G, changes Messiaen's A♭ to A♮,[15] and is laid out in fourths rather than thirds. But Scriabin's association of different transpositions of this chord with different colours seems to have been as different from Messiaen's synæsthetic perceptions as it was from Rimsky-Korsakov's.[16] Unfortunately, as a psychological phenomenon, synæsthesia has apparently been so rare among prominent creative individuals from generation to generation as to have evaded systematic research. In attempting detailed discussion of Messiaen's association of colour and harmony – 'when I hear music, ... I ... see inwardly, in the mind's eye, colours which move with the music'[17] – we are therefore largely thrown back on the composer's own attempts to describe it.

There is evidence of various kinds that specific colours and colour-combinations were associated in Messiaen's mind with specific transpositions of modes 2, 3, 4 and 6. The composer himself indicated this, in conversation with Claude Samuel:

> For me, the first transposition of Mode 2 [i.e. t0: C, D♭, ...] is defined like this: 'blue-violet rocks speckled with little gray cubes, cobalt blue, deep Prussian blue, highlighted by a bit of violet-purple, gold, red, ruby, and stars of mauve, black, and white. Blue-violet is dominant!' The same mode in its second transposition [t1: C♯, D, ...] is totally different: 'gold and silver spirals against a background of brown and ruby-red vertical stripes. Gold and brown are dominant!' And here's the third transposition [t2: D, E♭, ...]: 'light green and prairie-green foliage, with specks of blue, silver, and reddish orange. Dominant is green.' Mode 3 is four times transposable, but its best transposition is the second [t1: D♭, E♭, E♮, ...]. I even think the second transposition of Mode 3 is the best of all my modes. For its colors, I've noted the following: 'horizontally layered stripes: from bottom to top, dark gray, mauve, light gray, and white with mauve and pale yellow high-lights – with flaming gold letters, of an unknown script, and a quantity of little red or blue arcs that are very thin, very fine, hardly visible. Dominant are gray and mauve!'
>
> ... the modes have overall colors corresponding to their various transpositions (three colors for Mode 2, four colors for Mode 3, six colors for Modes 4 and 6), ...[18]

The American music theorist Jonathan Bernard has corroborated and extended this through extensive examination of Messiaen's writings and statements, together with analysis of his music.[19] Bernard's study of the piano's 'blue-orange' chords from the middle section of the 'Vocalise ...', however, suffers – as he himself acknowledges – from the difficulty of reconciling some of the most prominent chords with Messiaen's modes.[20]

Ex. 2.5 shows, in schematic form, a number of extracts from the piano's 333 continuous chordal semiquavers in *ii*/D:1–G:8. The entirety of the passage is put together on the basis of these little formulæ – shuffled and reshuffled, sometimes foreshortened, sometimes extended with transpositions of part or all of the formula. The dynamic level throughout is quiet, though this is not absolutely constant, as the piano responds within its own frame to the way in which the *vocalise* of

Ex. 2.5 Formulæ from piano part, *ii*/D:1–G:8

the violin and cello leads towards a *mf* climax at F:1. This climax is reached in the central section of the melody, which falls overall into three such broad spans of which the last (G:1ff.) is almost identical to the first. The kaleidoscopic permutations of the piano's formulæ do not follow this melodic reprise, however, nor do its occasional returns to fragment (a) serve to demarcate formal boundaries in its incessant tinkling. In all three instruments, though, the last two bars of the passage (G:9–10) present an echo of the end of the *vocalise*, and then an echo of the echo.

Looking more closely at the piano's 'gentle cascades', we may see in fragment (a) that the third and fourth chords are taken from the music of the very first bar of the faster opening section of the movement (*ii*/A:1), and that the first two chords of the fragment are the same but transposed upwards by a perfect fourth. Note that the transformation in rhythm from A:1 to D:1 is the exact obverse of the relationship we noted in Ex. 2.1 between the scurryings of the violin and cello at B:1ff. on the one hand and their serene *vocalise* on the other. Fragment (b) is cited by Messiaen in *Technique* as an example of chords of superimposed fourths, as is fragment (j); fragments (c) and (k) are shown as examples of the 'chord of resonance'; (d), he observes, lies in the second mode of limited transposition. Fragment (g), together with (a) and (b), is grouped with others from his works, without detailed technical comment, exemplifying 'connections of chords' in the 'natural harmony' which, he tells us, is 'voluptuously pretty by essence, willed by the melody, issued from it, pre-existent in it, having always been enclosed in it, awaiting manifestation'.[21]

We may note in addition that fragments (e) and (f) are closely related: the chromatic lines which move in contrary motion in (e) move downwards together in (f). Fragment (i) presents reduced versions of the 'chord of resonance'. Fragment (h) has an inverted pedal (the high F♮): below this a transposed version of the melodic sequence from fragment (j) is supported, as there, with parallel harmonies, though in fragment (h) these are built of thirds (inverted forms of the dominant ninth chord) rather than fourths. Finally, fragment (l) begins as fragment (j), before in its last four chords transforming music from *ii*/B:5 into a regular semiquaver rhythm (cf. the relationship of fragment (a) to A:1).

The evidence of colour associations with these materials is at first sight inconclusive. Neither pair of chords in fragment (a), for example, corresponds precisely to any of the modes that Messiaen associated with colours (i.e. modes 2, 3, 4 or 6), while the transposition of mode 2 found in segment (d) is that which he described to Claude Samuel as being dominated by gold and brown. The various 'chords of resonance' can provisionally be linked with colours through their association with mode 3 – and indeed Messiaen's association of his synæsthetic perceptions with phenemona of resonance would suggest it is here that the most certain examples of colouration might be found. We may note that in both fragments (c) and (k), the 'chords of resonance' fall into pairs, each with a common bass note, to give what Messiaen termed 'the ... effect of a stained-glass window' – or perhaps here the rainbow he mentions in his description of the movement. The inversional relationship between the two chords in each pair moves the underlying acoustic root by ic4, so preserving the same transposition of mode 3 as a close relative. But if any one form of mode 3 predominates, it is that associated with resonances on A and D♭ (and also F) – and this is the transposition of the mode that according to Messiaen is dominated by grey and mauve.

A further perspective on these 'blue-orange' chords comes through examination of the way Messiaen perceived certain colours as complementary. As Paul Griffiths has noted, Messiaen's usage of this term is in some ways problematic,[22] but in terms of 'vibrations' – through which the composer identified a connection between his colour perceptions and acoustic resonance – his pairing of blue with orange, red with emerald-green and yellow with 'pale violet or mauve' is logical, as these represent consistent 'transpositions' along the frequency-related scale that is manifest in the visible spectrum.[23] On this basis, one might expect the complement of orange to be what might be called a sky-blue, whereas the complement of gold (which lies between orange and yellow) would be a deeper blue. Messiaen also explained to Samuel that when a chord was transposed up an octave its colour was shaded towards white, and conversely with downward transpositions;[24] and this aspect of his synæsthesia might account for browns being found along with orange, gold or yellow, for example, and with greys appearing almost anywhere. In a later account of the *Quatuor*, Messiaen amplified the 'blue-orange' description, adding references to mauve, gold, green, violet-red and steely grey,[25] and one might certainly expect a wide range of colours to be repesented in a passage likened by the composer's marking to 'drops of water in a rainbow'.

This raises the prospect of a *reductio ad absurdum*, as it would seem to admit almost any colours, and to allow almost any modal or other acoustic explanation; but the weak representation of the red–green axis in all the evidence assembled remains striking, and is consistent with the original description of 'blue-orange'. Ultimately, however, while we can have no grounds for disputing Messiaen's account of his own perceptions, we cannot know just *how* he saw colours in this music.

3

Abîme des oiseaux

Clarinet solo. The abyss is Time, with its sorrows and its weariness.
The birds are the opposite of Time; they are our desire for light, for
stars, for rainbows and joyful songs![1]

Messiaen's interpretation of the scriptures here is illuminating, insofar
as it can be reconstructed from these brief remarks. Ian Matheson has
suggested that the 'abyss' refers to a passage in Revelation 11:7, in
which 'the beast that ascendeth out of the bottomless pit shall make
war against [the two prophets], and shall overcome them, and kill
them'.[2] This vision is treated more fully in Revelation 9:1–6, where the
abyss (or 'bottomless pit' in the King James version) is opened by the
fifth Angel of the apocalypse:

[v. 1:] And the fifth angel sounded, and I saw a star fall from heaven
unto the earth: and to him was given the key of the bottomless pit. [v.
2:] And he opened the bottomless pit; and there arose a smoke out of
the pit ... [v. 3:] And there came out of the smoke locusts upon the
earth: and unto them was given power ... [v. 4:] And it was commanded
them that they should not hurt the grass of the earth, neither any green
thing, neither any tree; but only those men which have not the seal of
God in their foreheads. [v. 5:] And to them it was given that they
should not kill them, but that they should be tormented five months ...
[v. 6] And in those days shall men seek death, and shall not find it; and
shall desire to die, and death shall flee from them.

Although one ought not to doubt that Messiaen's subject was indeed
the apocalypse, one can imagine that the words 'And to them it was
given that they should not kill them, but that they should be tormented five months' would have had particular resonances for his
fellow prisoners-of-war. As indeed might his own words: 'The abyss is
Time, with its sorrows and its weariness.'

Something similar may be said of the image of the bird. In Messiaen's programme note, the bird is presented almost as a Christ-figure, granting the hope of salvation. But in the literature and folklore of imprisonment, birds are seen as a symbol of freedom and hope in a different sense. It is in this absorbing movement for unaccompanied clarinet that we find the most explicit link between incarceration and 'the end of time'.

Rhythm

The movement falls into a number of sections defined by its changes of tempo:

A	*Lent* (♪ = c. 44)	13 bars, the last '*sans presser*'
B	*Presque vif* (♩ = c. 126)	6 bars
C	*Lent*	1 bar, '*sans presser*'
D	*Presque vif*	4 bars
E	*Modéré* (♪ = c. 92)	5 bars
F	*Lent*	12 bars, the last '*sans presser*'
G	*Modéré*	2 bars
H	*Presque vif*	1 bar, the last 4 notes '*Lent* (♪ = c. 100)'

The use of the word 'bar' here needs some qualification, since in this movement barlines seem to be used by Messiaen only as a point of psychological orientation for the performer. There is no time-signature, and the lengths of the 'bars' vary widely, some containing a single semibreve or minim, others extending to the length of 76 or 77 semiquavers (*iii*/D:4, F:11).[3] The rhythmic freedom which Messiaen instils into the unaccompanied melody is counterbalanced by a secure sense of form: B, C and D, together with the last bar of A, constitute a second section in two parts, giving the movement an overall shape which may be summarised as abc–a'c'–coda.

Messiaen's point of departure for this extended melody seems not to be plainsong, as it was in the second movement. Tracing the origins of some of his preferred 'melodic contours' in *Technique*, he draws comparison with phrases from music by Musorgsky, Grieg, Debussy, Russian folk song, plainsong and Hindu ragas, showing how his own

Ex. 3.1 (a) *iii*/A:1–5; (b) hypothetical four-bar tonal model in 4/4

(a)

p (désolé)

(b)

p (désolé)

melodies differ from them only through the application of his favoured modal shapes and rhythmic innovations.[4] Ex. 3.1 essays this process in reverse, for the sake of discussion. (It should be emphasised that there is no suggestion that Messiaen actually worked in this way, let alone that he worked with the actual substance of this example in mind – what is shown here is simply intended to give an indication of stylistic distance.) Ex. 3.1b[5] shows a four-bar phrase in common time; the phrase falls into two equal parts, the second of which matches the first in rhythm and answers it melodically at the cadence-point. Knowing Messiaen's identification of the initial melodic pattern with Musorgsky's *Boris Godunov*, one might imagine this as a Russian song, in slow tempo, supported by tonic and subdominant harmony in E minor that alternates on each crotchet beat. With such minimal harmonic movement one would imagine it to be the opening of a much larger melodic span, perhaps of sixteen bars.

Messiaen's own musical phrase from the opening of 'Abîme des oiseaux' retains some of these features: it is certainly the start of something much longer, and although the pitch materials are taken from mode 2 rather than E minor it could still be supported by a minimal harmonisation, such as that found in the passage from *La Nativité du Seigneur* with which he illustrates this melodic formula in *Technique*.[6] A first point of difference: like Ex. 3.1b, the phrase from 'Abîme des oiseaux' falls into two equal halves, the second of which answers the first; but the two halves are elided, with the second minim doing double duty by both ending the first subphrase and simultaneously beginning the second. Further differences concern the semiqua-

Ex. 3.2 *iii*/A:11, showing relationship between phrases

vers in Messiaen's phrase. As compared with Ex. 3.1b – which, let us not forget, is no more than a fabrication – the semiquavers are examples of 'added value' (*valeur ajoutée*): short notes which, as Messiaen explains in his preface to the score, are 'added to a rhythm, whether as a note [as in 'bars' 2 and 4 of Ex. 3.1a], as a silence, or as a dot [of augmentation]'.[7] The semiquavers in 'bars' 1 and 3 of Messiaen's melody doubtless spring from a similar rhythmic impulse; in terms of our fictional counterfoil, they might be regarded as examples of 'inexact diminution'.[8]

The entirety of section A is cast in mode 2, though the tonal focus on E is also clear, if not continuously so. For example, the 'dominant' note B receives emphasis at *iii*/A:9. Phrases within the section are set apart by breath marks and in two cases by rests. As the music develops, its rhythms become more supple and its melodic span reaches well away from the initial restricted group of pitches.

There is a fascinating relationship between the fifth and sixth phrases, as shown in Ex. 3.2 (note that Ex. 3.2b continues from where Ex. 3.2a leaves off). It is as if the second of these phrases is the model for the first – rather as with Ex. 3.1, though here entirely within Messiaen's own style. The first phrase lies a minor third lower in pitch, and interpolates a beamed group of four quavers after the initial group of three (notice that the dot of augmentation used at the outset of the second phrase is omitted from the first). The most intricate transformation now follows: the rhythm of the second phrase at (x) is augmented – that is to say, its note-values are doubled in length, as

43

shown between the staves. This rhythm is applied in the first phrase to the (transposed) pitch succession A♭–G–F, but the A♭ is played twice, as two quavers, rather than once as a crotchet. What is more, each of the first three quavers (A♭–A♭–G) is extended by means of an added value in the form of a semiquaver – these notes duplicating the melodic pitch succession a minor third *above* the version of Ex. 3.2b, rather than below. Finally in the first phrase, the motion from F to E is projected as a rising major seventh rather than a falling minor second, and this larger interval is filled in with a B♭, continuing the secondary melodic progression from D♮–D♭–C♭. All of this gives some inkling of the manner in which Messiaen's apparently fluid melody is carefully held together by internal consistencies.

Finally, a sustained E is reached in *iii*/A:13, animated not melodically or rhythmically but through a 'progressive and powerful' crescendo from *ppp* to *ffff* which acts as an anacrusis to the following *presque vif* section.

Birdsong

Each of the two principal *presque vif* sections (B and D) is introduced by the 'powerful' crescendo on a sustained E. They are thus cast together in a two–part song form, which is perhaps appropriate in that each begins with an imitation of birdsong. The music is marked 'bathed in sunshine, like a bird, very free in movement', recalling the association of birds with freedom discussed at the beginning of this chapter.

Messiaen's statement that 'the birds are the opposite of Time' might lead one to conclude that the birdsong music is set musically in opposition to the music of the slower sections. This is not necessarily the case, however, because the slower music, too, frees itself from the rigours of traditional musical time – albeit not in the transcendental manner of 'Liturgie de cristal' – as Messiaen himself indicated when he conceded in conversation with Antoine Goléa that the title of the *Quatuor* might contain a play on words concerning on the one hand the end of mortal time and on the other his hope for an end to 'the equal and measured time of classical music'.[9] There is contrast between the sections, of course, but also a sense of shared purpose.

Ex. 3.3 *iii*/B:1–3

The opening four 'bars' of the first *presque vif* constitute the first example of birdsong Messiaen gives in *Technique*.[10] Like the clarinet part in the second movement of the *Quatuor*, this passage combines elements of the two birdsongs – those of the blackbird and the nightingale – that are heard separately in 'Liturgie de cristal' (see Ex. 3.3). Since Messiaen was later to pride himself on his painstaking fieldwork in pursuit of birdsong transcriptions, one might wonder how 'accurate' the songs are in this piece. He can hardly have undertaken any field trips from Stalag VIIIA, after all, though he will surely have heard birds of some kind there.[11] Certainly, the birdsong passages in the *presque vif* sections peter out very quickly, giving way to flourishes based on the arpeggiated 'chord on the dominant' with double appoggiatura (see pp. 22–3). The first of these (from the end of *iii*/B:4) is also given as an example in *Technique*.[12]

The handling of the 'chord on the dominant' in this movement is inventive: in some instances the pentatonic group which lies below the pairs of fourths is truncated; the direction of motion can be downwards or upwards, or (as in the example given in *Technique*) one of these after the other; two forms of the figure can be elided together through a pivot note. The purest example, on the other hand, is isolated by the *pressez* marking at *iii*/B:6. In D:4, such figures go so far as to depart from their strict basis in an underlying chord, developing the flourish itself as a melodic configuration.

The first *modéré* (section E) begins with a strikingly varied form of the melody from *iii*/A:1 (Ex. 3.4). The music has moved to the 'dominant' of E, though once again this tonal orientation is expressed not by a diatonic key but by a version of mode 2, here transposed downwards by ic2 (the equivalent, because of the limitation on transposition that applies at each ic3, of a transposition downwards through a perfect fourth, that is, by ic5). The expected pitch sequence, then, is B–Eb–D–F–B–C–D, and indeed this is what is played. But the notes are

Ex. 3.4 *iii*/E:1

taken in different registers, ascending towards the highest reaches of the instrument and then descending. (Whether this is a pictorialism influenced by the image of the birds' flight is impossible to judge.)[13] The rhythm is transformed into even quavers and the presentation is *fortissimo*; an echo follows in the next bar. The rest of this section acts as a transition towards the expressive chalumeau register of the instrument, in which – exactly an octave lower than at A:1, and thus regaining the orientation towards E – a modified reprise of the opening material is heard.

After this, the 'powerful' crescendo leads not to a *presque vif*, but to a brief second *modéré* (*iii*/G:1–2). As did the first, it presents a form of the movement's opening melody transformed by registral changes, though inverted in contour. Again a *fortissimo* statement is followed by an echo.

Finally, there is a concentrated squib of a coda: the 'chord on the dominant' flourish is presented at the *presque vif* tempo, in its purest form but in retrograde (by comparison with *iii*/B:6). The figure is extended at the end into a chromatic descent which cues a fragment of the movement's opening melody (cf. A:1–2) – though now played *fortissimo* and marked with accents, transforming it into a brassy fanfare that brings us back into the realm of the apocalypse.

4

Intermède

A scherzo of more superficial character than the other movements, but linked to them nonetheless by melodic reminiscences.[1]

It would surely have been unthinkable for Messiaen to have omitted from the *Quatuor* this unpretentious little movement, which was composed initially as a free-standing piece for his three fellow prisoners (see pp. 7–8). Nonetheless, both its title and the composer's programme note confirm, by their failure to make any mention of the apocalypse, that the 'Intermède' stands outside the orbit of what was to become the work's greater inspiration.

Mood

If 'Abîme des oiseaux' presents a meditation on freedom and hope through an escape from 'the equal and measured time of classical music'[2] and an invocation of birdsong, the 'Intermède' is escapist in a contrasting way: it evades through its musical lightheartedness the sombre if uplifting reflections that occupy the remainder of the *Quatuor*. It does this in an exactly contrasting way, through its conspicuous use of regular rhythms and phrasing; and also – whilst it makes considerable use of Messiaen's modes – through its clear tonal orientation and formal layout.

Although Messiaen generally and most typically tackled lofty themes in his music, this is by no means the only piece he wrote that is lightweight in tone. (He would doubtless have recognised as a young man that his much admired teacher Paul Dukas, though a serious and self-critical composer, was nonetheless famously capable of humour in music.) Messiaen's *Fantaisie burlesque* for piano (1932) seems in its outer sections almost to be inspired by ragtime, even if the dreamlike

Ex. 4.1 Opening melodic phrase (*iv*/A:1–4), shown in relation to E major

reflection of its central section is entirely personal in tone and style. Yet more surprising is the brief *Rondeau*, also for piano, which Messiaen provided as a test-piece for a competition at the Paris Conservatoire in 1943 – only a short time after his repatriation from Stalag VIIIA – for this incorporates turns of phrase that even Francis Poulenc might have recognised as his own. It is noticeable, however, that Messiaen's characteristic fingerprints gradually encroach in greater quantity as the piece goes on.

Something of the kind can also be said of the 'Intermède', but overall it is a more consistent and satisfying piece than the *Rondeau*. Even the stylistic limitations within which Messiaen chose briefly to work did not prevent him from employing materials characteristic of his 'musical language', albeit in a less thoroughgoing way. The opening theme, for example, is cast in a jauntily off-key E major (Ex. 4.1a) which turns out to correspond to a form of Messiaen's mode 2. (The notation of Ex. 4.1a tilts the balance visually towards E major by making use of a key signature; performance indications are omitted.) The few notes that lie outside the E major scale are encircled in the example: but as Ex. 4.1b indicates, these notes are largely subordinated in the larger expression of an E major orientation by their placement in relation to the other notes. The A♯s are always cast as neighbour-notes to Bs, for example; and the D♮ in bar *iv*/A:4 is cast as an *échappée* from the diatonic note C♯ which is itself a neighbour to the B at this point, in a kind of inversion of the configuration involving A♯, G♯ and B at the beginning of A:3 (this is shown by the slurs in Ex. 4.1b).

The first F♮, and the F♮ in bar *iv*/A:2, are heard as straightforward passing notes between triadic pitches – something which Messiaen allows to happen by omitting the G♮ that would appear in the full version of mode 2, so that the motion E–F♮–G♯ can be heard as an alteration of E–F♯–G♯, for example. The second F♮ in bar A:1 demands further comment, however, for it is placed in a strong metrical position and cannot convincingly be understood as a lower neighbour to the G♯s that precede and follow it. The fact that it begins a three-note group that is a sequential variant of motive (x) signals the value of taking a slightly larger view, in which the E that begins (x) and the F♮ that begins the sequential variant are seen to be linked at a deeper level of the melodic motion. The prominent G♯ in the next bar completes an expanded (x) motive at this level (shown in Ex. 4.1b by a lightweight beam joining the three notes); looking further, we can see that the (y) pattern in the fourth bar (E–B–E, ascending) is likewise expanded at the next deeper level by a version of (y) that encompasses the entire phrase.

It is this clear tonal patterning – which when not at the surface of the music is to be found immediately beneath it – that distinguishes this melody's relationship with conventional tonality from that of, say, the melody of the first of the younger Messiaen's eight Preludes for piano, 'La colombe' (1929). In that melody, which also uses the transposition of mode 2 that is angled towards E major, the F♮ is frequently used as if it were a melodic substitute for the tonic pitch E rather than as a jovial displacement of a passing F♯. Nor does 'La colombe' have the exaggeratedly four-square rhythmic profile which is largely responsible for the lighthearted effect of the melody from 'Intermède'.

The melody shown in Ex. 4.1 is presented in bare octaves, as is its continuation into an eight-bar phrase. The music that follows from *iv*/B:1 begins by repeating the opening, but the music is varied from the third bar onwards. Harmony is introduced here for the first time, though it is not chordal but merely a thickening of the melody itself. There is a move to the dominant, reflected in terms of mode 2 by transposing it upwards by ic1 – which, because of the fact that the transpositions repeat at each ic3, is the equivalent of a downward transposition by ic5. This mode is the source of the neighbour-notes that decorate a two-bar prolongation of the dominant triad in B:3–4.

Ex. 4.2 *iv*/D:1–4, cello

p chantant

After this, there is a bar of subdominant harmony decorated by notes
from a version of mode 3 – though the modal basis is scarcely recognisable – before a return to the dominant at B:6 is expressed entirely
diatonically by a sequence of parallel triads.

At this juncture comes a contrasting section of five bars, led by the
clarinet. The flourish based on an arpeggiated 'chord on the dominant'
is played twice – each time within the confines of a single bar of 2/4,
and both based, as one might expect, on the dominant of E major.
Then a fragment of the blackbird's song is heard, accommodated not
only to the prevailing 2/4 metre but also to Messiaen's mode 1, the
whole-tone scale. In the next bar (*iv*/C:3), a descending form of this
scale (in the transposition that includes the note E) leads into a reprise
of the movement's opening tune.

Only four bars of this are heard, played by the violin. The cello acts
as a foil in *iv*/C:5–6, shadowing the violin a tenth below but itself
staying resolutely within the pitches of the C major collection. The
clarinet's counterpoint in the following two bars is based again on the
whole-tone scale.

The rondo-like pattern continues at *iv*/D:1 with a longer episode
which again links mode 2 with major-key tonality of the most straightforward kind. A four-bar melody is played with an accompaniment of
simple arpeggios: first in G major by the cello (Ex. 4.2), then in C
major by the violin, and finally in F major by the clarinet. In each case,
the transposition of mode 2 is used that matches the local tonality in
the same way that E major was matched in the opening bars. The G
major phrase, therefore, begins this section with the same transposition of the mode as was heard in the melody of Ex. 4.1. Another cross-
reference is the figure of five notes that ends the phrase, since this is
derived simply from the same juncture of the opening melody (A:8) by
doubling the note-values and transposing it to the new key.

Just as the G major opening of the section took its modal basis from

Ex. 4.3 *iv*/F:1–5, violin (cf. *vi*/A:1–2)

the larger E major, so the final F major – which has been reached by the simple tonal means of traversing the circle of fifths – is linked by a common transposition of mode 2 to the dominant of E major, which duly arrives at *iv*/E:3, after a two-bar link made up largely of scales based on the same mode. The clarinet's arpeggiated 'chord on the dominant' again leads at this point, though with more tonal movement than there was in the corresponding passage at bars B:7–C:3.

Notation

At *iv*/F:1 a new melody is played by the cello and the violin three octaves apart, the music of which looks quite different on the page from anything seen in this movement thus far (see Ex. 4.3). This melody lies fully within Messiaen's rhythm domain of 'added values' and so forth, but it is notated in the 2/4 metre of the movement and so on paper appears syncopated.

Messiaen himself acknowledged in *Technique* the necessity for compromise in notating his characteristic rhythms in certain circumstances.[3] He divided the solutions into four categories of notation, the first being that encountered in 'Abîme des oiseaux', in which 'the exact values [are written], without measure or beat, while saving the use of the bar-line only to indicate periods and to make an end to the effect of accidentals'.[4] The second and third notations are designed to answer the difficulties faced by orchestral musicians and need not concern us here, but the fourth is that encountered at this point in the 'Intermède':

> [This notation is] easiest for performers since it in no way disrupts their habits. It consists, by means of syncopations, of writing in a normal metre a rhythm which has no relation to it. This procedure is indispensable when it is a question of having performed by several musicians a superposition of several rhythms, complicated and very different from

each other. ... This notation is false, since it is in contradiction to the
rhythmic conception of the composer; but if the performers observe the
indicated accents well, the listener hears the true rhythm.[5]

Perhaps the most necessary use of the 'fourth notation' is in 'Liturgie
de cristal';[6] it is also fully evident in parts of the second and seventh
movements. But the present example is arguably the most striking, in
that the melody of *iv*/F:1ff. reappears as the principal material of the
sixth movement, 'Danse de la fureur ...', but is written there in the
'first notation' and so looks completely different on the page. If this
distinction seems in part to be the insignificant concern of mere score-
readers, one must not overlook the effect on performers, as Messiaen
makes clear both in his explanations in *Technique* and in the preface to
the score of the *Quatuor*. The latter also reminds us by implication that
his colleagues in captivity were inexperienced in his musical idiom and
must have needed coaching in its demands.

The final cadential figure of this free-floating melody (*iv*/F:8–G:1)
is echoed twice, the second echo being cut short by a return to the
material based on the clarinet's arpeggiated 'chord on the dominant'.
Here, recalling the 'stained-glass window' effect we have encountered
in previous movements, the initial note B – that is, the dominant of
this movement's overall tonal centre – remains constant: the chords
themselves, however, are based first on underlying diatonic collections
of D major and F♯ major, before E major is regained (albeit accompanied by scales of C major in the violin and cello).

Bars *iv*/H:1–8 and I:1–2 present an almost exact reprise of the
opening of the movement (A:1–8 and B:1–2), but the first four bars are
now harmonised using the full resources of mode 2. The reprise then
omits two bars, so that bars I:3–4 take up the music of B:5–6; this is
adjusted, however, so as to land not on the dominant triad but on that
of C major, which we have observed as a counterfoil to the tonic on a
number of occasions in the movement. A brief coda is unequivocally
based on the E major triad, which is strummed pizzicato by the string
instruments and even manages to constrain the final burst of song
from the blackbird.

Antecedent phrase of theme (*v*/A:1–6), showing motives (x) and (y)

majestueux, recuelli, très expressif

as shown in Table 5.1. As he points out, the middle part is
ionally long', and this is reflected in its internal division into
eriods.[8] The organisation of this section also exemplifies what
n calls 'commentary':

odic development of the theme ... in which some fragments of the
e are repeated in the initial key upon different degrees, or in other
and are varied rhythmically, melodically and harmonically.[9]

mple, the opening motive (x) of the theme, which at *v*/A:1
n B (see Ex. 5.1), is presented in varied statements in the first
f the middle section, on notes that form a descending arpeggio
D♯ at B:1, B at B:2, F♯ at B:3, and D♯ again at B:4, an octave
an at B:1. Similarly, the second period varies a motive from
wn as (y) in Ex. 5.1, which is presented on C♯ at C:1, on B at
on A at C:3.

5

Louange à l'Éternité de Jésus

Jesus is here considered as the Word. A long phrase for the cello,
infinitely slow, magnifies with love and reverence the eternity of this
powerful and gentle Word, 'which the years can never efface'. Majesti-
cally, the melody unfolds in a kind of tender and supreme distance. 'In
the beginning was the Word, and the Word was in God, and the Word
was God.'[1]

A number of commentators have expressed misgivings about the implications of Messiaen's transcription of this movement, along with
the final movement of the *Quatuor*, from earlier compositions in which
the music does not have the same verbal connotations. Paul Griffiths,
for example, observes that

> although it may be no great distance ... from seeing water as a 'symbol
> of Grace and Eternity' in *Fête des belles eaux* to conceiving the same
> music as illustrative of the 'Eternity of Jesus', the introduction of the
> Word can scarcely be dismissed as insignificant.[2]

Be that as it may, a closer look at Messiaen's description of *Fête des
belles eaux* suggests that the two conceptions were not so very different.
The work was composed as one of twenty commissioned by the City of
Paris at the time of the great international Exhibition of 1937:

> The City of Paris had organised an entertainment of sound, water and
> light, which unfolded on the river Seine at night ... The sounds were to
> be amplified by loudspeakers placed on all the buildings in the vicinity
> of the Seine, the *ondes* lending themselves marvellously to this open-air
> music [*musique de plein air*]. ... The night was mysterious, the deep
> water had a funeral aspect, the fireworks were gay, unconstrained
> trifles ... In contrast, the waterspouts were furious and awesome, or
> dreamy and contemplative. It was the latter sentiment that predomi-
> nated, and in the best moments of *Fête des belles eaux*, that is to say

when the water twice attains a great height, one hears a long, slow phrase – almost a prayer – which turns the water into a symbol of grace and eternity, according to the book of John: 'the water that I shall give him shall be in him a well of water springing up into everlasting life'.[3]

There can be no doubt – since most of the music of the *Fête* is redolent of 'gay, unconstrained trifles' – that the twice-heard 'long, slow phrase' is indeed the music that Messiaen transcribed into the *Quatuor*.[4] Its association with Christ's words (as reported by St John) immediately links it straightforwardly and unequivocally with the avowed subject matter of the 'Louange à l'Éternité de Jésus'.

One can well imagine how Messiaen might have felt, contemplating the memory of this pre-war Parisian scene, with its intermingling refractions of light and ethereal electronic sound, from the wilderness of Stalag VIIIA.[5] It is significant that he would later describe the work as 'musique de plein air', as if in direct contrast to his captive state when composing the *Quatuor* – rather as the birds provided a contrast which he preserved by transcribing their songs. The prayer-like melody is in fact heard twice in its entirety in the *Fête*: it is the first of these statements, for solo *ondes* with accompaniment in three parts, that is transcribed into the *Quatuor*, with scarcely any change apart from the articulation of the sustained accompaniment into the piano's slowly pulsing semiquavers – even the timbre of the solo *ondes* in the original is close to that of a solo cello (the accompanying parts are also string-like in tone). Given the inevitable rarity of the *Fête* in performance, however, it must be a cause for regret that Messiaen had no scope to transcribe instead the wonderful second statement, in which the melody and its accompaniment are transposed up a fifth to a scintillating B major and the two remaining *ondes* shadow every inflection of the melody with flute-like trills and harp-like arpeggios as if to make manifest the upper resonances of the melodic notes. Repeating their decorative figurations at each quaver, these two parts produce a wondrous evocation of sparkling water, which at the unearthly slow pace gives every impression of an eternal fountain.

That said, the first version is arguably more reverent in tone and thus more appropriate to its place in the scheme of the *Quatuor*. Coming after the 'Intermède', the function of this movement – akin to that of the opening 'Liturgie de cristal' – is as a kind of prelude to the

second act: renewing the focus on eternity which the apocalyptic personages and events that will re ing two movements. To this extent the 'Louange not engage in detail with the words of Revelation the Word, and the eternity of the Word, achieves

Song

In *Technique*, Messiaen cites the melody of this version for cello and piano – as the first of his two sentence'. Though arguably no more than a desc dy's formal outline, this lends new meaning to tl music with the Word: if this is a 'song' then without-words, but it is not Wordless. And it may of this melody from the *ondes Martenot* to the ta dium of the cello's upper register – in which, for e of the player's left hand on the neck of the instru audible alongside the musical notes – was comp with the theological fact of the Word made flesh.

Writing in detail of the 'song-sentence' and its siaen says that

> the song-sentence, cited by D'Indy in his *Cours* divided thus: a) theme (antecedent and consequent) inflected toward the dominant; c) final period, an iss

Under this scheme, and according to the example to present,[7] the melody of the 'Louange à l'Étern

Table 5.1 Formal structure of 'Louange à |

A:1–6	antecedent	theme (i.
A:7–12	consequent	
B:1–6	1st period	middle p
C:1–4	2nd period	
C:5–8	3rd period	
D:1–9	final peri	

Ex. 5.2 Conjectural reconstruction of 'missing' bars between *v*/D:3 and D:4

The melody of the final period is clearly related to the opening, though it starts on E (at *v*/D:1) rather than B and is expanded into a single nine-bar span. (The version in *Fête des belles eaux* includes two additional bars between D:3 and D:4; this passage is shown in Ex. 5.2 as it might have appeared in the *Quatuor*.) What marks this period out as a formal reprise, then, is not entirely a matter of melodic substance – since this is fairly consistent throughout the movement because of the nature of the middle section – but to a considerable extent the consequences of its tonal articulation. As Messiaen suggests in his outline of the 'song-sentence', the middle section is 'inflected' towards the dominant; the complement to this is a return to tonic harmony as a point of reference throughout the final period.

Tonality

The tonal architecture of this movement repays further analysis, not least because it emerges almost immediately that the relationship with Messiaen's modes is less straightforward than in the 'Intermède' or 'Abîme des oiseaux'. Here the tonal architecture is more developed, moving from the tonic region of E major towards the dominant – as Messiaen's description of the 'song-sentence' suggests – and also taking in motion towards the subdominant and onto the dominant of the dominant. At the same time, the modal component of the musical language includes not only mode 2 but also from time to time mode 3.

In *Technique*, Messiaen described the tonal potential of the modes by saying that

> They are at once in the atmosphere of several tonalities, without poly-
> tonality, the composer being free to give predominance to one of
> the tonalities or to leave the tonal impression unsettled. ... Thus mode
> 2 in its first transposition [here called t0: (C, Db, Eb, E♮, F♯, G, A, Bb)]
> can hesitate between the four major tonalities of C, E-flat, F-sharp, and
> A.[10]

Analogously, mode 3 at t0 (C, D, Eb, E♮, F♯, G, Ab, Bb, B♮) is by this reckoning 'in the atmosphere' of C major, E major and Ab major. It seems that when Messiaen wrote *Technique*, and indeed when he composed most of the *Quatuor*, his perspective on the relationship between the modes and what he called 'major tonality' had become quite clear. His 'musical language' employed the modes as a basis; and these had various possible tonal connotations which could be brought out by types of contextual emphasis: prominent melodic notes, root-position chords, rhythmic stress, etc. But in the two borrowed movements of the *Quatuor*, perhaps because they were composed a little earlier, the relationship between tonality and the modes is less easily described.

For example, the only transposition of mode 2 that includes the tonic triad of E major is t1 (C♯, D, E, F, G, G♯, A♯, B). The dominant triad is found in t2 and the subdominant triad in t0. Thus the correlation between the transpositions of mode 2 and the tonal regions of a stable key, such as E major in this instance, is in principle not too difficult to follow. With mode 3, however, it is different: the tonic triad of E major is found in the t0 form of the mode, which also contains the dominant triad;[11] but the tonic triad is additionally to be found in the t1 form of the mode (Db, Eb, E♮, F, G, Ab, A♮, B, C), which also encompasses the subdominant triad. Thus, motion among the primary regions of E major might be expected to shift less predictably between these forms of mode 3 than is the case with mode 2.

In the 'Louange à l'Éternité ...', the range of fluid connections between tonal areas and modal transpositions is indeed extraordinarily tangible to the ear, not least because the music's 'infinitely slow' tempo means that the journey from each note or chord to the next is weighed over a very long time by comparison with the normal pace of musical events. As Joel Lester has observed:

> reinterpretations of pitches and their interaction with the underlying harmony occur throughout the movement, imparting much of the intense expression of the movement. Throughout the movement, our hearing wavers between the tonal interpretation of local events and a nontonal perspective. The extremely slow tempo allows us to appreciate fully every one of these interactions.[12]

In this movement, it is as if the single tonality of E major is held in the 'atmosphere' of several modalities, rather than vice versa.

At the outset, the antecedent phrase of the theme (see Ex. 5.1) is presented with a strong E major orientation: the cello's expressive melodic line gives emphasis to the notes of the tonic triad, while the piano's supporting harmonic progression takes this chord in root position as its point of departure and return. But the recurring F♮s and G♮s in the cello part (v/A:1, A:2 and A:4) seem to be used in place of the F♯s diatonic to E major, and thus to be taken from a linked modal collection. The music of the piano strongly suggests that this is mode 2 (t1): its harmonies follow a sequence of major triads, some enharmonically spelled, with roots a minor third apart: E–B♭–G–B♭–E, and since this is the generating interval of mode 2 (see Appendix) the harmonic progression cues its presence here, as does the stepwise motion within the same mode of the topmost and lowest of the three triadic 'voices'.[13] The range of harmonies formed between the two instruments during the phrase embodies the modal–tonal interaction with greater richness, adding minor sevenths, major sixths and augmented fourths above the basic triads: each of these chord-types is also available in diatonic tonalities, but their appearance on E, G and B♭ rather than in conventional tonal relationships confirms the modal basis here. Mode 3 is latent in this passage only in the scarcely audible sense that the notes of the cello's opening descent (B, G♯, G♮, E, F♮ and C♯) are precisely those shared by mode 2 (t1) and the t1 (tonic–subdominant) form of mode 3. The cello cadences unequivocally in mode 2 at v/A:6, however, through the belated incorporation of a D♮ into the melody, achieving a sense of resolution as it does so.

Ex. 5.3 Harmonic outline of *v*/A:9–12

In the consequent phrase of the theme (*v*/A:7–12), the cello's melody is identical to that of the antecedent for the first four bars, and the piano's entry at A:9 is on an E major triad, exactly as before. After this, however, the harmonies differ, combining with the 'different melodic descent'[14] in A:11–12 to angle the music towards the dominant in anticipation of the middle section. This is shown schematically in Ex. 5.3. The first change comes with the piano's sequential motion onto a triad of F♯ minor at A:10. Whereas in the antecedent phrase the motion of the topmost and lowest 'voices' was by step within mode 2, here it is by step within the linked diatonic collection of E major. In terms of harmonic functions, the motion is from I to II. Above this chord, the cello melody descends from the diatonic ninth of the chord (G♯) to the seventh (E) by way of two passing notes (G♮ and F♮) which – as we have seen in the antecedent phrase – are taken from the tonic (t1) form of mode 2 and the tonic–subdominant (t1) form of mode 3.

The last three harmonies of Ex. 5.3 link the E major scale with different transpositions of both modes – namely the t2 (dominant) form of mode 2 and the t0 (tonic–dominant) form of mode 3. The modal collections have changed, but the referential diatonic collection has not: to borrow Tovey's well-known distinction, the music is 'on' the dominant rather than 'in' it. The cello's notes over these three chords indeed remain within the E major collection, climaxing on the dominant note, B. Above the first chord, the suspended melodic E resolves through the diatonic collection to D♯, combining at this moment with the piano in an enharmonically spelled dominant seventh on F♮ – a tritone away from B. This interval is utterly characteristic of mode 2 harmony: the F7 chord relates to the final chord of the phrase (B7 in the piano, forming B13 with the cello's G♯) in the same way as the enharmonic B♭ major triads in the antecedent phrase relate to the tonic triads of E major there, and all the notes involved lie within the t2 (dominant) form of mode 2. The intervening chord (C♮, F♯ and E in the piano, with B in the cello) may be interpreted tonally as a chromaticised II-functional chord, and modally as coming from the tonic–dominant (t0) form of mode 3. Thus, whereas the second and third chords rehearse the II–V progression with the first chord diatonic and the second replaced by a modal relative, the fourth and fifth chords present the progression with a modally chromatic II leading to a clear dominant chord.

As we have seen, the middle part of the 'song-sentence' is said by Messiaen to present 'fragments of the theme ... repeated in the initial key upon different degrees, or in other keys'. In the present context of linked tonal and modal resources, however, the meaning of these words is vastly expanded. It follows that the course of the modal–tonal interactions is likely to be difficult to follow in detail, and a complete analysis of the remainder of the movement in these terms would require the introduction of additional theoretical principles well beyond the scope of this chapter.[15] The opening sonority at v/B:1 presents a clear cue nonetheless: its characteristic mode 2 harmony of a major triad with superimposed augmented fourth (A, E C♯, D♯) strongly suggests the t0 (subdominant) form of this mode, to which the piano indeed adheres in its descending sequence of triads rooted a minor third apart (A, F♯, D♯) in B:1–3. The fact that the second of these triads is minor rather than major means additionally that in the first two bars the piano's notes lie fully within the E major diatonic collection. Nor is the third constituent in the network of collections, mode 3, absent from the mix, for the cello and piano together in the first bar of the period lie precisely within this mode in the corresponding tonic–subdominant (t1) form.

Among other clear indications of modal–tonal interaction in this part of the movement, perhaps the most significant is the fact that the bass line's dual membership of the E major collection and the t0 form of mode 2 continues as far as v/B:5; at B:6 it begins a chromatic progression from C♮ to F♯ (both of these pitch-classes being strongly implicated in the tonal associations of the same modal collection). The F♯ becomes in due course, at C:4, tonally functional as the dominant of the dominant (V of V), preparing for the third period of this middle part of the movement, during which the dominant is prolonged for four bars in preparation for the large-scale reprise in the tonic at D:1.

As might by now be expected, the first bar of the 'dominant preparation' (*v*/C:5) uses the pcs of the t2 form of mode 2, while the following three bars (C:6–8) remain strictly within the t0 (tonic–dominant) form of mode 3. But it is significant that the diatonic collection – whether of E major or B major – drops out of the picture at this point. Since in Messiaen's terms (and not only Messiaen's!) a modulation to the dominant key can be said to imply a change in the underlying diatonic collection,[16] the lack of diatonic reference in these four bars serves to neutralise the question of whether the music is 'in' or 'on' the dominant – a nuance that would be important in the case of a classically conceived dominant preparation beginning 'in' the dominant but ending 'on' it. Indeed, it is fair to say that the sense of large-scale return at this point of the movement does not come primarily from a sense of prolonged dominant harmony, but rather emerges from factors such as the rhetorical play of dynamics across the barline into D:1, the cello's melodic arrival on E♮, the piano's relaxation onto the tonic triad, the statement by the cello of a recognisable variant of the movement's opening theme, and probably some nuances of performance timing that serve to 'place' the downbeat gently but firmly. Nonetheless, the alignment in C:5–8 of the prevailing forms of modes 2 and 3 to the dominant of E major gives an underlying tonal logic to what happens at this juncture.

In the final period of the movement (*v*/D:1ff.), the cello's statement of the initial motive at last reaches the tonic note. As at the opening of the movement, the piano's harmonies are focused around the E major triad, though now in second inversion, and from this point until the end of the movement the notes of the piano part are taken entirely from the tonic (t1) form of mode 2. In contrast, the cello's melodic descent adheres to the tonic–subdominant (t1) form of mode 3, so that by comparison with the opening thematic statement the modal–tonal network has been expanded to encompass developments heard in the interim. But just as the cello's first statement clarified its allegiance to mode 2 as it arrived at a melodic cadence-point at A:6, so in its final ascent (D:7) the cello line incorporates an A♯, indicating its accommodation into the piano's mode. Indeed, from D:3 to D:6 the cello part inhabits both modes 2 and 3 simultaneously, just as it did (inaudibly) at the opening of the movement; here in the closing phrases, the ambiguity allows the music to move seamlessly from one mode into the other. The piano's previous use of the second inversion of tonic harmony gives the bass line scope to move steadily down to the tonic note, which it does by motion through the notes of mode 2 (B–A♯–G♯–G♮–F♮–E) rather than diatonically. At the same time the cello's rising arpeggio – which also, by virtue of the A♯, may be said to move through mode 2 – recalls part of the movement's dominant preparation (C:5), now appropriately transposed. At the very end, as the piano's repeating semiquaver rhythm is fragmented into stillness, the ringing clarity of the cello's high E, played as a harmonic of the open A string, brings an overwhelming sense of both E major and the note E itself as points of reference and tonal resolution.

6

Danse de la fureur, pour les sept trompettes

> Rhythmically the most characteristic piece of the set. The four instru-
> ments in unison are made to sound like gongs and trumpets (the first six
> trumpets of the apocalypse followed by various catastrophes, the trum-
> pet of the seventh angel announcing the consummation of the mystery
> of God). The use of added values, augmented or diminished rhythms,
> and non-retrogradable rhythms. Music of stone, fearful granite sonori-
> ties; the irresistible movement of steel, enormous blocks of purple fury,
> of icy intoxication. Listen above all to the terrible fortissimo of the
> theme in augmentation and the changes in register of its different notes,
> towards the end of the piece.[1]

In this 'dance of frenzy', there is no harmony to soften the impact of
the vigorous melody: all four instruments play the same line throughout – the piano in bare octaves and the others doubling as best they
can. Only in the climactic passage near the end (*vi*/O:1ff.) is this
limitation briefly transcended as the full range of the piano is brought
into play. Although Messiaen likens the extraordinary sonority of
the four instruments in unison to the sound of gongs and the seven
biblical trumpets, he perhaps wisely does not attempt to provide musical parallels to the 'various catastrophes' they announce. Instead, the
powerful tension of the instrumental unison is presented as an ana-
logue of these almost inconceivable events of judgement.

There is a residual parallel nonetheless between the musical form
and those passages of Revelation in which the sound of the trumpets is
described. After the fourth trumpet has sounded there is a brief moment of reflection from the writer of the scripture:

> And I beheld, and heard an angel flying through the midst of heaven,
> saying with a loud voice, Woe, woe, woe, to the inhabiters of the earth
> by reason of the other voices of the trumpet of the three angels, which
> are yet to sound! (Revelation 8:13)

Similarly in the music, after the first four statements of the principal theme there comes a middle section at *vi*/F:1, marginally less frantic, after which the material of the first part of the movement is taken up again with even greater velocity at I:1. It would be forcing the issue to attempt a correlation between the details of the music from this point onwards and the remaining events of Revelation 8–9, but there is certainly a sufficient quantity of restatement to make one believe that by the end of the movement the scene is set once more for the Angel who will announce the end of time itself.[2]

Texture

The unison texture of the 'Danse de la fureur ...' presents a fearsome challenge to performers. A wrong or even marginally misplaced note is immediately evident and can throw the whole ensemble off balance. The sense of strain engendered by the need to maintain this level of accuracy in an unrelenting melody of six to seven minutes' duration, cast in Messiaen's characteristically ametrical rhythms, is palpable even in the slickest of modern recordings. At the first performance in the prison camp the effect must have been electrifying. This is not to deny that all musical performance at the highest level is exacting; but this movement is a supreme example: the 'end of time' is evoked by the inordinate stretching out of the familiar moment of musical co-ordination into an unyielding span.

It may be that Messiaen had come across the extraordinary power of the full orchestral crescendo on a single B♮ at a climactic moment in the opera *Wozzeck* by Alban Berg, the score of whose *Lyric Suite* was among the few treasures he had with him in the camp. The effect of the unison in the 'Danse de la fureur ...' is not dissimilar, but the sheer length of Messiaen's music demands that this texture be articulated into far more than a single expressive gesture.

The principal theme has often been cited as an example of Messiaen's use of the 'added value' (see Ex. 6.1, in which the 'added values' are shown, as Messiaen does in *Technique*, with a + sign).[3] In terms of the feet of Greek prosody, an *amphimacer* is produced at (a) and (c), a *pæon* at (b) and an *antibacchius* at (d). From the perspective of the Western musical tradition, on the other hand, the principal effect of these isolated semiquavers is to prevent a regular quaver pulse

Ex. 6.1 Opening (*vi*/A:1–4), showing added values and Greek rhythms

from emerging: indeed, the first three bars would fall into 4/4 time if the added values were not present. The ear picks up a quasi-metrical articulation nonetheless, but it is one in which the 'beats' are not of equal length. Units of four, five and six semiquavers – beamed in Messiaen's notation as if they were the 'neumes' of plainsong – jostle together, allowing the sense of a four-bar pattern (2+2) to emerge with clarity, but never allowing the music to bowl along phrase-by-phrase in a way that might permit the listener to relax away from a perception of the very fast note-by-note pace.

The pitches of this phrase are within mode 6, but only one of them (B♮) lies outside the whole-tone collection (C, D, E, F♯, A♭, B♭), of which the D is not present. Since the B♮ is only heard twice, and then as a neighbour note or passing note, it is tempting to regard this theme as one of the composer's rare uses of mode 1.[4] This seems unlikely to have been Messiaen's conception, however, given the chronological proximity of the movement's composition to *Technique*, in which he specifically excuses himself from making prominent use of this mode, 'unless it is … unrecognizable'.[5] That said, he also fails to include this theme a few pages later when he cross-references examples of modes 4, 6 and 7 elsewhere in *Technique*.

The concluding phrase of the theme, shown in Ex. 6.2a, moves unambiguously to mode 2. Here there are still 'added values', but the ♫♩ ♫♩ rhythm of the first two crotchets recalls the 'Intermède' – a movement whose rhythmic profile for the most part stands deliberately outside Messiaen's ametrical style. (The exception in that movement is, of course, the premonition of the main theme of this one: compare Ex. 4.3 (p. 51) with Ex. 6.1.) Whilst the cross-reference to the 'Intermède' is clear enough within the context of the *Quatuor*, there is

Ex. 6.2a Continuation of theme (*vi*/A:5–6)

Ex. 6.2b Opening of 'L'Ange aux parfums' (*Les corps glorieux*)

also a fascinating comparison to be made with the opening section of
'L'Ange aux parfums', the third movement of the organ work *Les corps
glorieux* (1939). Ex. 6.2b shows the first eight bars of this section,
which is quoted in its entirety by Messiaen in *Technique* as an example
of a theme 'in which the added value … and Hindu melodic color are
united' – explaining that Hindu music 'abounds in curious, exquisite,
unexpected melodic contours which the native improvisers repeat and
vary following the rules of the raga'.[6] There can be no doubt that
Messiaen was sincere in his tributes to other cultures, as his use of
Śārṅgadeva's rhythmic formulæ illustrates, but this did not prevent
him from deploying exoticism at a point in the *Quatuor* where fantasti-
cal and catastrophic events are alluded to without close examination.

Returning to the musical comparison, it should be noted that the
tempo of the passage from 'L'Ange aux parfums' is much slower –
Modéré, un peu lent – than that of the 'Danse de la fureur'. On the
other hand, this entire melody, which lasts for two minutes in Messiaen's own recording,[7] is played alone without harmonic accompaniment, as is the melody from the *Quatuor*. It is clear that the first bar of
Ex. 6.2b (the music of which is repeated in the third bar) is a model for
the beginning of the second bar of Ex. 6.2a. In a similar way, the first
bar of Ex. 6.2a is derived from the final legato phrase of Ex. 6.2b. The
difference between the two passages comes about through a change of

mode: the collection (C, D, E♭, F, G, A, B) in 'L'Ange aux parfums' is exchanged in the 'Danse de la fureur …' for the mode 2 collection (C, D♭, E♭, F♯, G, A, B♭). This use of modal substitution to transform one theme into another does not seem to have been commonplace in Messiaen's work, but its use here supplies a fresh perspective on the respective discussions in chapters 3 and 4 on the opening themes of 'Abîme des oiseaux' and the 'Intermède'.

Shape

The material of the first part of the movement (up to rehearsal letter F) is based on four statements of the thematic material shown in Exs. 6.1 and 6.2a. The shape of this section may perhaps most readily be conveyed by the fact that the third statement of the theme (*vi*/D:1–6) is identical to the opening statement (A:1–6), whereas both the second and fourth statements truncate the first four-bar phrase to two bars but expand the concluding phrase into a wide-ranging melody. In these expansions the rhythm tends towards constant semiquavers, still articulated into groups of various lengths rather than falling into regular patterns. As well as the theme itself, there is the by now familiar shape of the arpeggiated 'chord on the dominant' with double appoggiatura – at C:1 (from the 12th note), C:2 and E:6 – together with some linking material based in part on small motives either taken from the theme or introduced into the expansion of its concluding phrase.

The central section of the movement (*vi*/F:1ff.) is dominated by non-retrogradable rhythms and a repeating cycle of sixteen pitches. The barlines in Messiaen's notation separate each non-retrogradable rhythm from its predecessor: bars F:1–7 present a sequence of such rhythms, of which the fifth and sixth are identical and the seventh a variant; this sequence is duplicated in G:1–7 (see p. 4). The seven rhythms contain respectively 5, 5, 7, 11, 9, 9 and 11 notes – so that the repetitions of the cycle of sixteen pitches (D–A–F♯–C♯–G♯–A♯–C♯–D♯–B–F♯–C♮–G–E–F♮–A–B♭) fail in every instance to coincide with the rhythmic boundaries from one to the next. In fact the complete pitch cycle is repeated seven times, and the first two notes are played for an eighth time in order to reach the conclusion of the rhythmic sequence.

Ex. 6.3a Regular note values: *vi*/I:1–3

ff non legato, martelé

Ex. 6.3b Augmentation of amphimacric rhythm: *vi*/I:4–5

bronzé, cuivré

fff

The last bar of this music builds climactically in even semiquavers – the pitches momentarily recalling the chord of resonance on C♯ (though inverted, with G♯ in the bass) – before presenting in *vi*/H:1–4 four successive downwardly-arpeggiated 'chords on the dominant'. These follow the sequence familiar from the opening of 'Liturgie de cristal' (see pp. 22–3), here with a constant F♯ in the bass. After this a codetta-like statement of the third and fourth bars of theme (H:5–6, cf. A:3–4) brings the section to a close on a sustained F♯.

The next section (*vi*/I:1ff.) is a kind of recapitulation of the first, but the music is rhythmically altered, sometimes re-ordered, and constantly interrupted. At I:1–3, the music of the opening theme (A:1–4, last two notes missing) is presented almost as if it were no more than a pitch sequence to be played in regular semiquavers (Ex. 6.3a); the occasional quaver values articulate the phrase, but not at the same points as before. This is the model for the transformation of other passages in the subsequent music: at J:1, K:1–3, L:1–3 (from B:3–C:2), and finally N:1ff. (from E:6, but extended into a great climax). The four arpeggiated 'chords on the dominant' from H:1–4 are also heard again, divided between I:6 and M:7 – their rhythm of even semiquavers now all of a piece with that of the transformed material from the first section.

The first interruption to this sequence of recycled material is shown in Ex. 6.3b. The pitch sequence F–C♯–A is played in a long–short–long amphimacric pattern, which is augmented and diminished variously – its shape remaining constant but expanded or contracted in length.[8] In the second bar, for example, the outer notes are ten semi-quavers in length and the central note five. A great variety of augmentations and diminutions is seen at *vi*/J:2–5 and K:4–9. The last two instances develop the pattern by registrally expanding it; when it next appears at M:8–9 the notes are trilled vigorously, and it is this that provides the basis of the climactic end to the section at N:9–14. One tiny detail of synthesis in the midst of all this juxtaposition and inter-cutting of material is to be found in bars M:1–6, where what appears to be a transformed restatement of the theme – along the lines of Ex. 6.3a – becomes rooted in the opening bar, in the process focusing on the motive B♭–C–A♭, which has the rhythm ♩ ♪♩♪ . Messiaen nicely points up the fact that this is a version of the amphimacric rhythm of Ex. 6.3b by presenting it in augmentation at the end of the phrase.

The last sixteen bars of the movement present the greatest spectacle, though they appear in the position of a coda. The sequence of events paraphrases the broad sequence of the movement: first comes a statement of the theme, then an allusion to the middle section (*vi*/P:1, cf. F:1) followed by the four arpeggiated 'chords on the dominant' (P:2–5, cf. H:1–4), with the two final bars recalling the ending of the first section. It is the first of these reminiscences, the climactic statement of the theme at O:1–9, that has received the greatest critical attention, and to which Messiaen refers in his preface when he writes of 'the terrible fortissimo of the theme in augmentation and the changes in register of its different notes' (Ex. 6.4). In *Technique*, Messiaen suggests that his model for this was Berg's *Lyric Suite*, a score he

Ex. 6.4 Changes of register: *vi*/O:1–4, piano

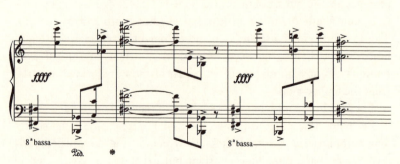

had with him when composing the _Quatuor_ (see p. 1).[9] A clear example of the same procedure in the Berg work (also a quartet, incidentally) may be found at bars 25–7 of the first movement; a more expressive use of constant registral changes to lend expressive power to a melodic line is the _arco_ entry of the first violin at the end of bar 6 of the last movement. In Messiaen's _Quatuor_, the effect is as much one of fragmentation as of heightened expression, fully conveying the sense of terror and power he evidently intended.[10]

7

Fouillis d'arcs-en-ciel, pour l'Ange qui annonce la fin du Temps

> Certain passages from the second movement return. The mighty Angel appears, and above all the rainbow which crowns him (the rainbow: a symbol of peace, wisdom and of all sounding and luminous vibrations). In my dreams, I hear recognised chords and melodies, I see known colours and forms; then, after this transitory stage, I pass beyond reality and submit in ecstasy to a dizziness, a gyratory interlocking of superhuman sounds and colours. These swords of fire, these flows of blue-orange lava, these sudden stars; this is the tumult of rainbows![1]

This climactic movement is the only one in which contemplation is subordinated to the depiction of events in a definite sequence. The principal musical consequence is that the formal structure of the music acquires something of the teleological quality that we associate with the sonata principle in the Austro-German tradition. But Messiaen's own description of the form – 'variations of the first theme, separated by developments of the second'[2] – makes it clear that his conception falls short of the dialectical interplay of themes and tonalities that post-Beethovenian sonata form frequently embodies. Nonetheless, the very idea of 'development' alerts us to something that distinguishes the treatment of themes in 'Fouillis d'arcs-en-ciel ...' from, for example, the linkage through complementary aspects of plainsong between the melodic materials at *ii*/B:1–3 and D:1ff. in 'Vocalise ...' (see pp. 29–31).

Developments

The comparison with the second movement is particularly germane because, as Messiaen makes clear, much of its material reappears here. This in itself causes attention to focus on the way the material is

Ex. 7.1 Opening of theme (*vii*/A:1–3, cello)

handled, rather than on its intrinsic qualities. The first theme – the one that is 'varied' rather than 'developed' – is new (Ex. 7.1), but it recalls the theme of the second movement's central section in a number of ways (*ii*/D:1ff.; see Ex. 2.1a, p. 30). The tempo of the two themes is identical, as is the constant semiquaver rhythm in the piano in both passages; the opening interval of the two themes is the same (though inverted), and they share a number of neume-like rhythmic nuances, notably the *bacchius* foot (short–long–long) introduced by the first 'added value' (see (a) in Ex. 7.1). The *forte* dynamic at *vii*/A:1ff. represents a marked difference, however,[3] and by comparison with the 'impalpable, distant' quality of *ii*/D:1ff. there is here a sense of common purpose about the two instruments: both are firmly within mode 2 – the same transposition is adhered to during the entire twelve-bar thematic statement – and the underlying harmonic motion in the piano part shadows the cello closely. The characteristic ic3 of mode 2 is used to link the phrases of what Messiaen terms 'a complete sentence'[4] (the opening three bars are restated, albeit transposed, and the final six bars present a balancing phrase); each phrase ends on a chord of the added sixth, rooted successively on A, F♯ and E♭.

This tightly coherent block of thematic material is well suited to a certain manner of variation: that is to say, where the shape of the theme remains essentially intact, though it may be decorated by ornamental notes or countermelodies, and its harmonic support may be paraphrased or presented in a different figuration. This type of variation technique, which is familiar from the works of Mozart and Schubert, stands in contrast to the principle of thematic 'development', and it is notable that Messiaen deliberately exploits this opposition in order to create a musical form – whereas composers of the Schoenberg school, following the precedent of Brahms, sought to compose with a technique of 'developing variation' in which thematic material was constantly transformed as if to create a musical argument or narrative.[5]

The second theme of this movement, which Messiaen tells us is treated by development, is taken directly from the second movement. To begin with, at *vii*/B:1–3, two passages from the opening of the 'Vocalise ...' (shown in Ex. 2.4, p. 34) are concatenated; then, from the end of B:3, fragments from the long succession of piano chords in the central section of the same movement are introduced (see (h) and (i) in Ex. 2.5, p. 37). This mixture of materials from two highly contrastive sections of the second movement unites them under a single tempo; indeed, at $\lrcorner$ = 66, this is somewhat faster even than the *modéré* of *ii*/ A:1, and very much faster than the *presque lent* of *ii*/D:1. The two components are also united in rhythm by an extraordinary sleight of hand on the composer's part, in which the incorporation of regular semiquaver movement into the material from the *modéré* is counterbalanced by the incorporation of longer note values into the material from the central section (see Ex. 7.2).[6]

In fact, the regular semiquaver pulsing – familiar not only from the piano's 'blue-orange' chords in the central section of the 'Vocalise ...' but also from the scurrying version of the plainsong-like melody at *ii*/ B:1ff. and from the piano figuration at the opening of the seventh movement itself – continues unabated in the eight bars between rehearsal letters *vii*/B and C. This tendency towards regular motion, set against Messiaen's characteristic rhythmic fluidity, may be likened to the Schoenbergian effect of liquidation:[7] here, it generates a constant tension as the highly differentiated rhythms are everywhere confronted by their nemesis, the 'equal values of duration' that Messiaen wished his *Quatuor* to bring to an end.[8] We have observed a preliminary exploration of this compositional strategy in his treatment of the main theme in the sixth movement (p. 69). And it is this theme which now reappears at *vii*/B:5–8 in the violin and clarinet, with its rhythm completely liquidated to regular semiquavers.[9] At the same time, the cello's *col legno* clattering in open fifths picks up the rhythm of Ex. 7.2, whilst the piano plays melodic patterns in mode 5 together with parallel three–note chords moving scalewise in mode 6.[10]

At *vii*/C:1 the regular semiquavers are interrupted as the piano plays five successive flourishes based on the 'chord on the dominant'.

the insistent off-beat syncopations that symbolise confidence for Handel (oboes and second violins in D major, less persistent syncopations for oboes alone in F). The grandeur of the scheme beats most of the other movements in *Water Music*, and for performers taking the 'salad-bar' approach to selecting a suite from this material, it makes an ideal finale (as both Hamilton Harty and Stokowski realised; see p. 123).

If the hefty Hornpipe is not have too terminal an effect, something lighter and more refreshing must follow. The French might have called the untitled **WM13** a 'Menuet à la sarabande' (the accent falling on the second beat of every other bar) and it carries the aura of a ballet or theatre borrowing. The sound of 'Travers e Viol I' on the top line is new, but the player(s) probably not; the *traverso* flute would have been played by most oboists of the period, or it could have been written for the trumpeter Grano and his 'German flute'. *RSM*, *Shaftesbury* and *Arnold* ask for 'Traversi' in the plural, but *Lennard* has 'Traversière' which is certainly singular.

The dance is perfectly simple in construction, made of 2- and 4-bar units only and with sufficient ambiguity to avoid the total seriousness of a sarabande, but with none of Henry James's 'twaddle of graciousness' that sometimes afflicts the minuet. This exquisite number has all the expressiveness of an aria but a wider range and more disjunct intervals than a voice would find agreeable; the lingering 4–3 French cadences in bars 38 and 40 are a last-minute expressive gift. There is no indication in any source to countenance a flute solo on repeats, simply the amorously softened sound of the violin line.

Two boisterous **Bourrées** or rigaudons interrupt the mood. *Aylesford* marks **WM14** Presto and *Arnold* and *Chrysander* call it Aria, suggesting another borrowing. Whether winds are involved or not is unclear: the *Aylesford* copyist kept the top stave for the 'Travers' as in the previous number, *Walsh* (followed by later editions) suggests oboes doubling (although the Violin II part goes out of range), and for the second dance *Aylesford* suggests the intriguing sonority of 'Hoboe I & II, Viola, Fagotto' for the four lines. No source suggests a da capo of 14 after 15, and it can be treated as a separate piece, unless the move from G minor to D major is thought too harsh.

The **Lentement (WM16)** has a strange pedigree and one of the few apparently original tempo markings of the whole suite. Its essentials can be found in Keiser's *Claudius*, a 'macaronic' opera of 1703 with some arias in

Ex. 3.13

Ex. 3.14

Italian and some in German: a chorus of Bacchantes sing 'ô Evan Evoë' (Act 3, scene 8) with 'satyrs, and women playing tambours and cymbals' celebrating the grape harvest. But this (presumably fast) 12/8 gigue over a drone bass is far removed from what Handel made of it (see Ex. 3.13).

Handel visited this movement twice: in 1734 it served in the *Pastor Fido* Act I ballet music as a 'Danse Pour les Chasseurs', to which it is indeed better suited. But here, reduced to a slow gigue loure and with the trumpets where one might have expected *traversi*, it strikes the ceremonial mode of Mouret or Lalande. J. C. Smith, a normally reliable copyist, calls it a 'Marche Lentement' in *Granville*, which is presumably a slip, unless Handel intended a slow march, one-in-a-bar. A wind band of some size (*not* a solo trio) is needed to deliver the requisite presence for bars 19 and 20, in alternation to the strings. If the bowing pattern suggested by Georg Muffat (*Florilegium secundum*, Passau 1698) for a slow gigue is adopted a marked articulation is felt at each bar-line (see Ex. 3.14).

In Handelian terms, the blunt (untitled) **Bourrée** (**WM17**) spells 'finale'. Almost identical phraseology, innocent rhythms, and the curt ending of bar 4 are found in such music as the final Coro of *La Resurrezione*, where the abrupt cadence is a setting of the exclamation 'Viva'. The arrangement for two horns in *Forrest Harmony* (see above, p. 30) is marked 'Presto', although there is no tempo marking in other sources. In outline the piece can be traced to a movement from *Daphne* (HWV 352), and perhaps in Handel's private plan it signalled the end of an internal sequence, as numbers 3, 9, and 12 had done previously. Smith's specially emphatic final bar-lines may be coincidental. Walsh's 1733 parts, but no earlier sources, suggest 'This Aire to be play'd thrice'; if adopted, the scoring would presumably be varied as in the three versions of the final movement (22).

From the **Menuet** (**WM18**) onwards each number presents a new instrumental colour. Here the bassoon is mentioned for the bass line in *Aylesford*; *RSM* and *Shaftesbury* give 'Bassoni e Violoncelli' and Arnold's source proposed 'Bassoni. Violonc.' without double bass, an interesting variant for this dark-coloured linear melody. *RSM* suggests '2 Fois' and both *Granville* and *Shaftesbury* give 'Twice', but there are no options for alternative scoring.

WM19, also in G minor, pursues the opposite melodic path, with featured leaps, and adds 'Flauti piccoli' to the top line, notated in C minor, a fourth higher than the violins' part. This was normal practice for the descant recorder (*Aylesford* calls it 'Flautino'), which sounded then a fifth higher still, i.e., an octave above the violins. Since they are specified in the plural, a shrill effect was obviously intended, but Handel would have been rightly shocked to find an orchestral piccolo allocated to this duty today. The echoes of a Viennese waltz are anachronistic but inevitable, helped by the evocative suspended sevenths in the harmony of almost every second bar. The bass line is calculated to delineate these complex harmonies without continuo assistance, but the extra note in the melody of bar 4 reiterates an ugly fourth against the bass. This is surely an early miscopying of a dotted minim (as in all other occurrences: bars 2, 10, 12 etc.), where the unclear dot was read as a note-head, and now is sanctified by every modern edition (but not the contemporary keyboard version HWV 539b). Alternatively, as in the 'Oxford' version (see below), bar 2 may also read as minim + crotchet, which at least imposes congruence on these phrases. *RSM* and *Granville* again give '2 Fois' or 'Twice' for this movement, but possibly to indicate the da capo of bars 1–16; the form is probably AABA, but AABBA is another solution. Nothing suggests a da

Ex. 3.15

capo of the previous number. An interesting earlier form of this minuet has been identified in Lord Danby's lute book, for which the terminal date is mid-November 1710; here we find the same outline of melody and descending bass in a Menuet included in a group of known Handel pieces but unattributed.[11] There would seem to be a direct line of descent from this version through the keyboard version (HWV 375 and 434) to the *Water Music* form, adding to the suspicion that this is a suite of pre-existing pieces, in some cases worked up from keyboard dances (see Ex. 3.15).

The overall increase in contrast observed throughout *Water Music* now reaches a level of caricature in the last two bucolic dances, with extremes of high and low tessitura (*Caricatura* or *Stravaganza* would have been the opposite of the *perfidia* noted in WM8). Handel repeats the device that he had used so effectively for the character of Polyphemus in *Acis*, the bass voice of the 'thund'ring Giant' ridiculed by his obbligato of a 'flauto piccolo'. The descant recorders are at the top of their register for the first **Country Dance** (**WM20**, so titled in *Granville*, with 'Alternativement' and 'twice' added, also in *RSM*). This is a brisk jig, where the bass line is given to violas (in fact it never goes below violin G) with 'Violonc.' (one or more?) doubling. The awkward upward leap in bar 7, where the violins at least could more naturally have continued descending in unison to bottom G, must have been adopted to keep the high tessitura. The choice of an overtly English jig (as opposed to a French *gigue*) is just as obviously a national gesture here as Haydn's quotation of 'Lord Cathcart's Jig' in the finale of his 'Military' Symphony, also designed to flatter the English taste.

WM21 is the obverse, major in place of minor, a melody on the bottom string for violin II and viola plus bassoons, and a bass line going down to bottom C. The effect would be comfortable and warming in any period, even without modern echoes of 'The Teddy Bears' Picnic' or even 'Pop goes the Weasel'. It is unclear why the bassoons and strings diverge in bar 5, when the bassoon top A could have been avoided by simply playing the last note of the bar an octave lower; faulty copying at an early stage may be suspected. Walsh's keyboard arrangement of this number, and also of the similarly scored central section of WM7, gives the violin I descant and bass only, but tactlessly omits the prime melody. The da capo question here is ambiguous. Smith heads the pair of dances 'Alternativement' but then adds a firm 'Fine' after 21 (it is the final number in the *Granville* sequence). Maybe the 'twice' against 20 leans in favour of a da capo.

Composers from Beethoven onwards looked to the final movement to consummate the whole construction but the eighteenth century was not 'finale-driven' in this way. Handel and his contemporaries would opt for a more abstract style of rounding-off a work – a fugal texture for a sacred piece, and frequently a deliberately nonchalant and catchy ensemble for an opera. In fact, Handel's opera finales (usually called Coro) often give the impression that the cast have already begun to drop out of character

Ex. 3.16

in the interests of providing a smooth re-entry for the audience to the real world. A minuet, the most calming and classless of dances, could do the same job for a suite or a pre-classical symphony. Several of Handel's minuets which rounded-off overtures became more popular than the overtures themselves (*Berenice, Arianna*).

The **Trumpet Minuet (WM22)** that closes the sequence of *Water Music* maintains royal grandeur of scoring – a true courtier never turned his back on the King – but is deliberately short-phrased and calls up again the repeated notes and trills that were first heard from the horns in WM3. *Malmesbury, Drexel, Arnold* and *Chrysander* title it 'Coro' without explanation, suggesting it had at one time existed in the opera-house, and in fact it turns out once again to be indebted to Reinhard Keiser; an 'Aria en Menuet con tutti li Stromenti' for Celinde, 'Ach Liebe bilde dir dieses nicht ein' in *Der angenehme Betrug, oder Der Carneval von Venedig* (1707) shows more than a nodding relationship with the trumpet line and its repeated notes (see Ex. 3.16). Handel however improves both melody and bass.

Was it a private joke on Handel's part to end his water entertainment with a borrowing from *The Carnival of Venice* as once presented in Hamburg? Would the King, or members of his family, or perhaps Baron Kielmansegge have recognised it? *Granville* and *Lennard* (but not *RSM*) suggest '3 times, 1st Trumpets & Violins, 2nd Horns & Hautboys, 3d all toghether [sic]' – a prolonging device we will later find in *Fireworks Music* – possibly as a safety measure, to be implemented if the royal party was still lingering. Here 'Violins' means all strings, 'Hautboys' full winds.

There are many later transformations of select movements from *Water Music* as songs and minuets (see p. 120). These adaptations are patently the work of other hands, but the recently published 'Oxford' version of *Water Music* is more enigmatic and deserves special mention alongside the other basic sources.[12]

This version formed part of the library of Richard Goodson, who was Professor of Music at Oxford from 1718 until his death in 1741, and it was probably used for performances that he directed in the 1730s. It consists of ten movements, including one that is now the minuet in Op. 3 no. 4, scored in four parts: two violins, bassoon and basso continuo, all in its correct *Water Music* keys. As a whole it makes a convincing suite, and some of its differences of detail make useful comparisons with the full orchestral text.

In the Air (WM6), which opens the suite, it gives essentially the version with the added horn, well represented by bassoon; there are more ties where other texts give repeated notes. For WM7 we have a better reading for the bassoon in bar 47. WM8 ends with a bare fifth in this version, and therefore expects continuo. WM16 is supplied with dynamics and WM17 has a decorated version of bar 11. WM18 is given with Violin I as the top line and Violin II taking the viola part; bar 18 is simplified, and again it ends with an open cadence, where the original has the middle part drop awkwardly to the third. WM19 gives the extra third beat in bars 2 and 4 (another way of solving the problem of non-congruence). The 'DC' at the end, as in other sources, means a repeat of the first section of 19, rather than a return to 18. In WM21 bar 5 is more congruent between bassoon and strings in this chamber version. In WM22 bars 9ff. the second violin part is set higher, a better choice than that given in the full score where the wide gap between the parts produces an unconvincing texture. Here and in WM16 there are usefully varied dynamics given for repeated phrases.

4

The 'indebtedness' of Handel

If ever there was a truly great and original genius in any art, Handel was that genius in music; and yet, what may seem no slight paradox, there never was a greater plagiary. He seized, without scruple or concealment, whatever suited his purpose. But as those sweets which the bee steals from a thousand flowers, by passing through its little laboratory, are converted into a substance peculiar to itself, and which no other art can effect, – so, whatever Handel stole, by passing through the powerful laboratory of his mind, and mixing with his ideas, became as much his own as if he had been the inventor. Like the bee, too, by his manner of working, he often gave to what was unnoticed in its original situation, something of high and exquisite flavour. To Handel might well be applied, what Boileau, with more truth than modesty, says of himself –

Et meme en imitant toujours original.

(Uvedale Price, 'Essay on Decorations', in *Essays on the Picturesque as compared with the Sublime and the Beautiful*, London, 1796)

Handel begins his *Water Music* suite – by most standards a very 'original' creation – with a borrowed style of Overture and ends with an 'influenced' Minuet. Throughout the previous chapter we have seen his reliance on pre-existing material (Porta, Keiser, his own chamber music), sometimes radically recast, sometimes adopted literally, often merely alluded to. Is this, or was this, a legitimate composing method? If so, how are we to explain it?

Many unsuspecting listeners are disturbed to find that much of their favourite Handel repertoire – music ranging from the so-called 'Largo' to 'I know that my Redeemer liveth', through *The Arrival of the Queen of Sheba* and even the opening of the Hallelujah Chorus – is, to some degree, indebted to other composers for its germ material. It is probably the widespread and lifelong nature of Handel's many tiny borrowings that makes the discovery more disconcerting than the milder surprise of discovering that *the* Toccata and Fugue in D minor is probably not by Bach or that the 'Albinoni Adagio' contains rather less than 2 per cent Albinoni. More space has been devoted in Handelian literature to the 'why?' of his borrowing than the 'how?' of his composing. In his own century this predilection for the use of pre-existing material was well known and seen by many as a method rather than a misdemeanour. Only later did it become a moral malady, and nowadays a musicological magnet.

Mattheson in 1722 hints at Handel borrowing from his *Porsenna*, but does not mention him by name. As he puts it, 'all elaboration, beautiful as it may be, is only interest: but the invention itself compares to the capital'. Mattheson agrees nevertheless that both parties can benefit from borrowing: indeed one can gain 'extraordinary honour, if a famous man now and then happens upon his track, and – as it were – borrows from him the very basis of his ideas'.[1] This uncensorious attitude to 'borrowing' is repeated throughout the century.

The Abbé Prévost (1733) enthusiastically supported Handel's methods for the good light the appropriations shed on his sources: 'some critics accuse him of having borrowed the substance of an infinite number of good things, from Lully, and above all from our French cantatas, which he has the skill, they say, to disguise as Italian: but the crime would be slight, were it certain: moreover, when one considers carefully the many works that Mr. Handel has composed, it is hard to imagine there would not be anything found there from the compositions of others'.[2] In a footnote, the Abbé, like Mattheson, sees this as 'trading up': 'This does honour to our musicians without doing harm to Mr. Handel.' In Germany, Scheibe acknowledged that both Handel and Hasse made use of material from Reinhard Keiser: 'they understood, however, the art of making these inventions their own, so that they were transformed in their hands into new and original ideas'.[3]

Charles Jennens, after showing off some of his new MS acquisitions from Italy, complained dyspeptically that 'Handel has borrow'd a dozen of the Pieces, & I dare say I shall catch him stealing from them; as I have formerly, both from Scarlatti & Vinci',[4] but he was concerned more about violations of his own library of manuscript scores than open plagiarism or compositional short-cuts. The commonly held English view was expressed by Charles Burney at the time of the 1784 Handel Commemoration: 'All that the greatest and boldest musical inventor *can* do, is to avail himself of the best effusions, combinations, and effects, of his predeccessors: to arrange and apply them in a new manner; and to add his own source, whatever he can draw, that is grand, graceful, gay, pathetic, or, in any other way, pleasing.'[5]

Professional colleagues saw the process in its most positive light. William Boyce put it tersely: 'He takes other men's pebbles and polishes them into diamonds', and William Crotch in a letter to Burney declared: 'the greatness of his mind, the accuracy of his judgement, the variety of his styles & skill in adopting the thoughts of preceding & coeval composers. – Bird might be as sublime, Hasse as beautiful – Haydn more ornamental – But Handel united grandeur, elegance & embellishment with the utmost propriety, & on this account I ventured to pronounce him, upon the whole, the greatest of all composers.'[6] This description owes more than a little to Sir Joshua Reynolds' famous commendation of Raphael, as the 'foremost of the first painters', explaining that 'the excellency of that extraordinary man lay in the propriety, beauty and majesty of his characters, the judicious contrivance of his Composition, his correctness of Drawing, purity of Taste, and skilful accommodation of other men's conceptions to his own purpose'.

Later writers became more censorious of such 'accommodation' – a reflection of the prevailing moral code rather than any greater insight into Handel – and 'borrowing' was assumed to be freighted with guilt. Sedley Taylor in *The Indebtedness of Handel to Works by Other Composers* (1906) and E. J. Dent (*Handel*; 1934) use a range of metaphor from moral delinquent to manic depressive. There was even a misguided attempt to save Handel from damnation by proving that he himself was the true author of the material he appropriated (Percy Robinson defending *Israel in Egypt* in *Handel and his Orbit*, 1908), another variant on what E. P. Thompson calls 'the enormous condescension of posterity'.[7]

Today the more relaxed image is that of the bee or the 'architect in sound', and there is intensified interest in how the material was put to work. Dealing with genius, it is never easy to explain the part of the recipe which involves *inspiration*. In Handel's case, it is simpler to track the *perspiration* – the work process – in large part because as an eighteenth-century craftsman he would no more have felt that he was restricted to material of his own invention than a cookery-book writer (of any century) might feel obliged to reject all pre-existing recipes.

The sheer range of borrowed material in Handel's compositions can be deduced from the variety of names mentioned in the few quotations above: Lully, Scarlatti, Vinci, Mattheson, Keiser. Almost every week more echoes of 'pre-existing material' come to light in Handel's works from every period of his career. The earlier theory (or excuse) that it was forced on him as a result of ill health, or mental breakdown – the mental and physical collapse of 1737 postulated by E. J. Dent – dissolves when it is discovered that Handel used this technique from his earliest days in Germany. John Roberts suggests that 'we must now conclude that in all probability Handel normally composed on the basis of old material during the last third of his creative life',[8] and Ellwood Derr, after discussing the source material for *Solomon*, written only nine months earlier than *Fireworks Music* and where 50 per cent of the movements use borrowings from a single Telemann source (*Harmonischer Gottes-Dienst*), decides that if this work 'is so permeated with foreign ideas, it would be rash to assume that any other work of Handel is wholly original'.[9] The subject is now so weighted down with literature (what a mis-typing has just described as 'extra-musical overtomes') that we may wonder how we are meant to respond to these 'disclosures'.

For a start, 'borrowing' (*Entlehnung*) is probably the wrong word, being strongly loaded with moral and legal resonance.[10] We must distinguish between a full, recognisable 'theme' and a commonplace 'motive' or trivial 'motto'; then there is the distinction between outside borrowings and self-borrowings; we must allow for subconscious memory, after long experience playing other people's music that shared a common language; and finally there could be open borrowing in the spirit of competition.

If we hunt for an explanation rather than press for a conviction, Mattheson's mention of Handel's early problem with 'air' could explain the root of this behaviour. Mattheson remembered that when he first met Handel at the age of eighteen, in 1703, 'he was strong at the organ, stronger than Kuhnau in fugue and counterpoint, especially *ex tempore*, but he knew very little about melody till he came to the Hamburg operas ...'[11] Handel's cure seems even then to have been an omnivorous appropriation of the widest range of germ ideas, which he then developed in the manner of a German improviser. His training had been that of a normal Lutheran organist – improvising on a known theme or chorale, and preluding on a figured bass outline. As an improviser, you don't *wait* for inspiration to strike, you begin with what you have and a *routine* ensures that you continue, expecting inspiration to arrive as you proceed. In this, cliché is a prop, not a problem. Forty years on from this basic training, Mrs Delaney remembered that Handel's favourite 'ignition' theme when extemporising after dinner on her harpsichord was the subject of 'And with His Stripes', in fact a commonplace of eighteenth-century fugal writing and scarcely differing from any other German organist's use of a *cantus firmus*. It is a nicety not to be overlooked that *because* of his borrowing and the fuss generated, we are in a much better position to assess Handel's technical genius, making it more illuminating to pass on to the 'how' of Handel's working methods with this material, rather than the 'why' and 'where' of its origins.

Unlike Haydn (or Liszt or Debussy), Handel does not appear to have used a ground plan of specific harmonic proportions; we find no Fibonacci numbers or Golden Ratio, nor any scribbled calculations in the margins of the manuscript as we see in Mozart. The total number of bars in a piece appears to be his only calculation, and that was after the event, to assist the copyist. Handel's sketches show local incidents rather than master plans, small fragments deployable to different contexts in a sort of *ars combinatoria*, and the visible contractions and expansions show experiment in progress. Sometimes Handel is even unaware of how many bars are needed for an insertion without experiment (see *Fireworks* MS, fol. 2lr and pp. 111–12 here). Unlike Bach, whose initial ritornelli took the most crafting and show the most alterations, since almost everything following was drawn from them, Handel's beginnings often lead to unexpected developments, and we find him turning back to an opening tutti to insert thoughts that were generated at a later stage.[12] Handel's actual working manuscripts provide our only evidence for the process, but these are graphic enough. Had he kept a working diary, we would probably find that he began, like his trumpeter John Grano, with a 'grand plan' subdivided into several 'moods'.

Grano, who may have played the trumpet in *Water Music*, was also a composer proficient enough to be published by the astute John Walsh; amongst other pieces he had his own 'Water Music' (first mentioned in

Ex. 7.2 Rhythmic realignment of materials

(a) *vii*/B:1–2 (cf. *ii*/A:1–2, piano)

(b) *vii*/B:3–4 (cf. *ii*/E:5–6, piano)

The last of these is taken up by the ensemble in a trilling texture at
C:3–4, with the appoggiaturas trilling downward to their resolutions –
G♮ to F♮ in the violin and D♮ to C♮ in the piano – as the cello spans the
sonority with siren-like glissandos between the same top G♮ and a B♭ in
the middle register. Underneath this, the piano strikes a bass chord
containing the three pitch-classes missing from the music above it (B♮,
E♮, A♮), in a manner reminiscent of the effects of resonance heard in

the *modéré* passages in the opening section of the second movement (see pp. 32–4) at *vii*/B:1–3. The remaining two bars of this thematic group (C:5–6) resume the constant semiquaver rhythm, taking as their point of departure the first eight 'blue-orange' chords from *ii*/D:1 (cf. (a) and (b) in Ex. 2.5, p. 37).

The presentation within this thematic complex of materials previously characterised by highly differentiated speeds, but now heard in close succession at a unified tempo, highlights Messiaen's extraordinary handling of tempo in his music. It is as if the musical material is conceived outside any temporal realisation, and that its speed of presentation – *presque vif*, *modéré*, *presque lent* or whatever – is simply applied to it in order that it may be made audible. This recalls Messiaen's pride in the separation of pitch and rhythmic patterns that he achieved in the work:

> one very important peculiarity of my music and of this quartet, is that, like Guillaume de Machaut [d. 1377] whose example I did not know at the time, the rhythms are dissociated from harmony and melody.[11]

The result of all this conceptual separation of musical elements and attributes is that the presentation of ideas in audible musical form is achieved by a converse process of combination and recombination. As we have seen, the construction of the second theme of 'Fouillis d'arcs-en-ciel ...' is itself achieved in this way through the concatenation of fragments from elsewhere under the umbrella of a new tempo and a constant semiquaver pulsing; at *vii*/B:5–8 there is in addition a superimposition of different musical ideas within the ensemble texture. These compositional devices recall aspects of Classical and Romantic music – specifically, motivic working and counterpoint – but there are important differences. When themes or motives are combined in counterpoint, in the works of Brahms or Schoenberg for example, the materials themselves are considered malleable and their note-by-note details are generally adjusted to meet various harmonic circumstances or the requirements of recognised musical forms. Messiaen's method of combination and recombination, on the other hand, normally keeps the materials themselves intact and conceptually separate. Various analogies to this practice may be offered, such as mosaic-work or the construction of a stained-glass window; in music, the closest precedent is probably not Machaut at all but the much more recent example of Stravinsky, whose music is famous for its block-like formal structures.[12] In his own analysis of Stravinsky's rhythmic working in *The Rite of Spring*, Messiaen found this principle to operate at a bar-by-bar level, and he acknowledged its influence on his own musical thought.[13]

All of this has significant consequences for the 'development' of the second theme as the movement proceeds. The next section, however, as demanded by the overall form, is a simple variation of the first theme (*vii*/D:1–12), which is characterised by the exclusion of the theme's first protagonist, the cello, from the texture. Its music is given instead to the violin, and both the theme and its piano accompaniment are transposed down by ic3, thus preserving the same version of mode 2 as before. Meanwhile, the clarinet plays gentle countermelodies, scalar for the most part, in the same mode, ending at D:12 with a flourish on the 'chord on the dominant' that leads into the new 'developmental' section based on the second theme.

What ensues, however, is not a section in which the materials played in bars B:1–C:6 are reworked. The opening of the section at E:1 is certainly in correspondence with B:1, but from the second crotchet of E:2 the music cuts immediately to the eight 'blue-orange' chords previously heard at C:5, near the very end of the thematic complex, and then continues with other material taken from the central section of the second movement but which has not so far been heard in this movement at all (cf. (g) in Ex. 2.5, p. 37). Then, after the second element of the theme has been played at E:5 (cf. B:2–3), other material from the 'Vocalise …' – though now from its first section – is played by the piano in E:6ff. (cf. Ex. 2.3, p. 32). As Messiaen points out in *Technique*, the violin, clarinet and cello parts at this point are based on the first eight 'blue-orange' chords, played in retrograde.[14] As the section continues, there are further cross-references to the second movement, but there is also some treatment of the various materials in ways that are recognisably developmental. These include a variant of the theme's opening at F:4, a hocketing rhythmic interplay between the piano and the other instruments at F:6–7, and repetitions of a melodic fragment with changing harmonies – Messiaen terms this a 'harmonic litany'[15] – at F:1ff.

Programme

The next variation of the first theme (*vii*/G:1–6) includes an arabesque figure in the piano, based on the pitch sequence of the concluding phrase of the theme of the sixth movement (*vii*/G:1 and G:4, cf. *vi*/A:5). Like the melody – presented in fragmentary fashion by the clarinet – this arabesque lies within mode 2, as also do the violin's arpeggios and the remainder of the piano texture. The cello again plays *col legno*, supporting the clarinet with the regular semiquaver rhythm that is by now an established feature of this movement. The appearance of material borrowed from another movement in a 'variation' rather than a 'development' section is significant in terms of the movement's overall shape, as is the fact that this variation uses the tempo of the *second* theme rather than that of the first. This marks a significant juncture in the progress of the movement towards a climax: an intermingling of attributes and elements of the two thematic groups that continues in the next 'developmental' section at *vii*/H:1ff.

Whilst it is probably futile to attempt a detailed correlation of this musical section with Messiaen's programme note, it is noticeable that what he writes there is also remarkable in its description of the climactic phase: the manner of expression is both unusually personal[16] and graphic in its imagery, suggesting a departure from the composer's normally unflappable equilibrium in dealing with theological events of apocalyptic proportions. Something of the same sentiment is to be found in his statement in the preface that 'All this remains a stammering attempt if the crushing grandeur of the subject is considered!'[17] Virtually the only straightforward image in the climactic phase of Messiaen's programme note is of 'blue-orange lava', which may readily be associated with the reappearance of the 'blue-orange' chords from the second movement. Elsewhere, the imagery evokes a synæsthetic overwhelming of the senses: the 'tumult' of rainbows, the rainbow symbolising 'all sounding and luminous vibrations', the dizzyness and gyration, the 'interlocking of ... sounds and colours'.

The increasing accumulation and superimposition of musical materials perhaps represents this rather better than a conventional thematic 'development' might have done. Bars *vii*/H:1–4 take the music of B:5–8 and add to it a violin counterpoint based on the rhythm of the first

Ex. 7.3

(a) Opening theme in regular rhythm (*vii*/J:1–2, cello)

(b) *vii*/J:1–3, clarinet

theme;[18] the piano's scalewise three-note chords are now played in the ubiquitous rhythm of constant semiquavers. At H:5ff. the reprise continues with the piano's 'chords on the dominant': here again the counterpoint based on the rhythm of the first theme is added (violin, clarinet and cello), and at I:1–2 (cf. C:3–4) the complementary notes (B♮, E♮, A♮) are not merely left in the resonating bass register but are taken up into the trill itself. A variant of these bars follows (C:6–7) after a bar of 'blue-orange chords' combined with their own retrograde. At J:1ff. the piano, starting with a return to the music of B:3–4 (see Ex. 7.2), continues with material adapted from the central section of the 'Vocalise ...', much as before. But again there is an accumulation of superimposed materials: both the cello and violin present the pitch sequence from the first theme of this movement in regular note values (the cello's version is shown in Ex. 7.3a),[19] while the clarinet – explicitly representing the 'dizziness' of Messiaen's programme note – plays the flourish based on the 'chord on the dominant', going first in one direction then another, in the palindromic manner of a non-retrogradable rhythm (Ex. 7.3b). All of this, and more, builds through a long crescendo to *fff* at K:1, where the final variation of first theme begins.

If the composer's intended effect is conveyed, then it is surely in part because of the sheer quantity of materials, the details of which are likely to elude even the most attentive listener:

Let us now think of the hearer of our modal and rhythmic music; he will not have time at the concert [i.e., while listening] to inspect the nontranspositions and the nonretrogradations, and, at that moment, these questions will not interest him further; to be charmed will be his only desire. And that is precisely what will happen; in spite of himself he will submit to the strange charm of impossibilities ... which will lead him progressively to that sort of *theological rainbow* which the musical language ... attempts to be.[20]

At the same time, the fact that the final variation of the first theme (vii/K:1ff.) regains the pitch level of the opening, and amounts to a clear restatement of the theme played forcefully in octaves by the violin, clarinet and cello, lends this moment the character of a thematic and tonal recapitulation – just as one might expect after a conventional development section. Both the constant trilling of the melody notes and the piano's arpeggiando figurations simply add to the effect of a grand reprise, rather than a variation, at this point – complementing the 'developmental' character of the immediately preceding music. These two things conspire to allude strongly to teleological musical structures at exactly the point where, in the overall programme of the work, the pivotal moment occurs. But as time is brought to an end, Messiaen's complex conception of the eternal is revealed once more as the music apparently turns full circle, briefly taking up the opening of the second theme at L:1 (cf. B:1) before being brutally interrupted – so that only silence remains.

8

Louange à l'Immortalité de Jésus

A long violin solo, acting as a pendant to the cello solo of the fifth movement. Why this second eulogy? It is addressed more specifically to the second aspect of Jesus – the man Jesus – to the Word made flesh, resurrected immortally to grant us life. It is all love. Its slow ascent towards the extreme high register is the ascent of man towards his God, of the Child of God towards his Father, of the deified Being towards Paradise.[1]

This movement is transcribed directly from the second movement of the early organ work *Diptyque* (1930). The subtitle of that work – 'essay on earthly life and blessed eternity' implies that it too is concerned with the transformation from mortal to immortal life. And since the section which is transcribed in the *Quatuor* is clearly the 'essay on ... blessed eternity', it requires little reinterpretation in its new context beyond making the Christian source of the blessed state explicit – as if it were ever subject to doubt – in the title of the movement.

There are few discrepancies between the organ score and the transcription, apart from the substitution of a hypnotic ♪♪ :: rhythm in the piano part for the sustained notes of the original organ writing. The music is transposed up a major third from C major to E major, matching the explicit tonality of the fourth and fifth movements of the *Quatuor* and the clear tonal centre of the third.[2]

Tempo

Like the fifth movement, this 'Louange à l'Immortalité ...' is cast in an extremely slow tempo – *extrêment lent* is the composer's own marking – which Messiaen associates with a state of ecstasy. The metronome marking of $\flat$ = 36 is in fact significantly slower than that of the corresponding section of the *Diptyque*, which is $\flat$ = 58. Whereas the marking for the *Diptyque* suggests an overall duration for the movement of around 4′17″, the score of the *Quatuor* suggests something close to 7′00″, and Messiaen's recorded solo performance of the *Diptyque* allows 9′22″.[3]

It is as if Messiaen's conception of this music were slowing down as he grew older.[4] Nonetheless, the *Diptyque* is far from being the only work to illustrate that extremely slow tempo markings had been characteristic of his music from the outset. His first mature organ piece, *Le banquet céleste* (1928), and the first section of his early orchestral work *Les offrandes oubliées* (1930) are marked *très lent*, and the final section of the latter work shares the *extrêment lent* and the $\flat$ = 36 of the 'Louange à l'Immortalité ...'. Many further parallels could be drawn from Messiaen's other works of the 1930s, among them the fourth movement of *L'Ascension*, 'Prière du Christ montant vers son Père', the subject of which is close to that of the final movement of the *Quatuor*, and the music of which is also marked *extrêment lent* ($\flat$ = 40). And within the *Quatuor* itself, the fifth movement outdoes all of these examples in its tempo of *infiniment lent* and a metronome marking equivalent to $\flat$ = 22.

Resolution

Messiaen's programme note makes it clear that this last movement is to be heard in contemplation of an eternity in which the tensions surrounding the events of the apocalypse have been resolved through the ending of time. His choice of music with a clear and simple overall form and readily perceived tonal architecture – as compared, most obviously, with the previous movement – must be understood in this context. It would be possible to read this as a tacit admission that his most recent style was less suited than that of a decade earlier to the expression of eternal peace. But the music is not out of line with Messiaen's 'musical language', for it makes significant use of the second mode of limited transposition; its rhythms, however, are devoid of the added values and other innovations Messiaen brought to his rhythmic language during the later 1930s.

Table 8.1 Interaction of mode 2 and E major collection in *viii*/A:1–6

	C	C#	D	D#	E	F	F#	G	G#	A	B
viii/A:1–3		C#	D♮		E	F♮	F#		G#	A#	B
mode 2 (t1)		C#	D♮		E	F♮		G♮	G#	A#	B
E major		C#		D#	E		F#		G#	A♮	B
viii/A:4–6	C♮		D♮	D#	E		F#		G#	A♮	B
mode 2 (t2)	C♮		D♮	D#		F♮	F#		G#	A♮	B
E major		C#		D#	E		F#		G#	A♮	B

As in the case of the fifth movement, however, Messiaen's principal citation of the 'Louange à l'Immortalité …' in *Technique* concerns its form. He describes the movement as a 'binary sentence', falling into the following sections:

(a) theme [*viii*/A:1–6, see Ex. 8.1]
(b) first commentary, modulating more or less, inflected toward the dominant of the initial key [B:1–9]
(c) theme [C:1–6]
(d) second commentary, concluding upon the tonic of the original key [D:1–11][5]

The term 'commentary', as we have seen in chapter 5 (p. 56), refers to a thematic development based on one or more fragments of the theme: in this case, the fragment is that shown at (x) and (y) in Ex. 8.1 (*viii*/A:3 and A:6).

The theme itself falls into two three-bar phrases, in the second of which the melody is simply transposed downwards by ic2. This transposition, however, does not at first sight seem to accord with the change of harmony: the opening phrase is supported by a tonic triad with added sixth, and the harmony at *viii*/A:4–5 (including the prominent A♮ in the violin part) is a dominant minor ninth. Closer examination reveals that the music exemplifies interaction between the diatonic collection and mode 2, similar to the multi-collection interaction that we have seen in the fifth movement. The pitch collection found in A:1–3 is (C#, D♮, E, F♮, F#, G#, A#, B); in A:4–6 it is transposed downwards by ic2 to (C♮, D♮, D#, E, F#, G#, A♮, B). As shown in Table 8.1, these collections are virtually identical to mode 2 (i.e. octatonic) collections t1 and t2 respectively: in each case, one

Ex. 8.1 Opening theme (*viii*/ A:1–6), showing motive (x)

Ex. 8.2 *viii*/B:1

octatonic pc is missing and one non-octatonic pc is added.[6] As we have noted in other movements, the transposition of an octatonic collection downwards by a perfect fourth (ic5) – corresponding to the interval between tonic and dominant – is identical to its transposition downwards by ic2, which is precisely the interval of transposition applied to the near-octatonic collection seen here. E major remains a fixed point of reference as the harmony progresses from tonic to dominant, and it is in the E major collection that the non-octatonic notes (F♯ in A:1, E♮ in A:4) may be understood to originate. Thus, although the strong tonal focus initially suggests that this is tonal music with occasional chromaticisms that derive from mode 2, there is perhaps greater justification in saying that it is essentially in mode 2, with 'chromatic' pitches derived from E major.

At the opening of the first 'commentary' the octatonic basis is further transposed downwards by ic2, corresponding to a move from the dominant to the subdominant. Within each of the two bars *viii*/B:1 and B:2, there is a local harmonic progression to the tonic triad, decorated by an added ninth (F♯) and an oscillating melodic motion between the tonic note E and a diatonic neighbour note, also F♯. These two aspects of the music are illustrated in Ex. 8.2. In Ex. 8.2a, the notes enclosed in the area (x) are from mode 2 (t0) and the notes in area (y) are from the E major collection (C♯ and D♯ are missing from both collections; note that the F♯ is common to both). Ex. 8.2b views this passage from an E major perspective rather than in terms of collections, showing how the neighbour group (C♮, A♮, G♮) resolves chromatically to elements of the decorated tonic triad; the arpeggio-like group E–G♮–B♭ is only to be explained in relation to mode 2,

Ex. 8.3 (a) adapted from *Technique*, Vol. 2, Ex. 249; (b) *viii*/B:6–7, piano

however – an octatonic arpeggio, as it were – but it has of course already been established as a melodic motive in the preceding phrases.

At *viii*/B:3 the violin begins a slow, weaving ascent – further developing the same motive – which from the middle of B:3 until the end of B:5 is supported by chords deriving entirely from mode 2 (t1).[7] As the violin reaches the top of its ascent (a still higher peak will come towards the end of the movement), the piano plays what Messiaen terms a 'harmonic litany', in which the two-note sequence B♮–A♮ is repeated with two different harmonisations.[8] The thickened piano texture to some extent obscures this effect: Ex. 8.3 presents a schematic comparison of the piano part with a transposed version of the corresponding example from Messiaen's *Technique*. The final chord of this pattern is voiced as a dominant-quality chord with the tonic note unresolved within it, and this is prolonged (with embellishments) throughout the next three bars (B:7–9), ending the 'first commentary' with an inflection towards the dominant, as Messiaen prescribes.

The second statement of the theme follows the first exactly (*viii*/C:1–6), and the first two bars of the second commentary also continue as before (D:1–2). At this point, the violin's second ascent begins: as Messiaen points out, it starts from a lower point (middle G♯ rather than the B♮ above) but attains a higher goal.[9] As before, its harmonic support lies within mode 2 (t1) from the middle of D:3 until the end of D:5 (corresponding to B:5), at which point the first commentary's obscure 'harmonic litany' is replaced by the clearest of tonal cadential progressions, departing from mode 2 (t1) at D:6 and resolving back into it at the moment the tonic triad is reached by way of a perfect cadence at D:7 (see Ex. 8.4). In the last five bars of the movement, the

Ex. 8.4 *viii*/D:5–7, showing interaction of mode 2 and functional harmonies

violin finally reaches towards the pinnacle of its ascent: E in the highest register of the instrument. The piano prolongs the tonic harmony, moving within it not by way of the notes of the E major scale, however, but through the notes of the 'tonic' transposition of mode 2, thus bringing these two elements of Messiaen's musical language into equilibrium at the close.

9

Contexts

The *Quatuor pour la fin du Temps* is among Messiaen's best known compositions, and has been recorded many times. Possibly out of respect for the extraordinary circumstances surrounding its composition, it seems to have been more or less immune to the harsh criticism that from time to time beset the composer and his works. Another protective factor may have been its unusual format: as a piece of chamber music it is not quite unique in Messiaen's output, but it remains the case that works for orchestra, piano, organ or voices comprise over five-sixths of what he wrote, and those who sought to make critical arguments for or against the composer's highly individual and characteristic style were perhaps unlikely to direct their attentions to a work that might have seemed peripheral by comparison with, say, the *Turangalîla Symphony* (1946–8) or the vast piano cycle *Catalogue d'oiseaux* (1956–8).

Public trajectories

In the period following the composition of the *Quatuor* and his repatriation to occupied France in the spring of 1941, Messiaen set about his work with remarkable vigour. Later the same year he took up an appointment at the Conservatoire as professor of harmony, and in the following year he set about writing *Technique de mon langage musical*. He also returned to composition, although the works he wrote initially were either brief or unfinished, namely the *Chœurs pour une Jeanne d'Arc* (1941, unaccompanied voices), the *Musique de scène pour un Œdipe* (1942, *ondes Martenot*), and the *Rondeau* (1943, piano). In addition to his pedagogical work at the Conservatoire, Messiaen began in 1943 to teach a private class in 'formal analysis, orchestration, rhythm, melody, and harmony of all kinds of music: classical, romantic, ancient, exotic, and modern'.[1] This class met at the home of Guy Bernard-Delapierre, whom Messiaen had got to know briefly in the transit camp near Nancy, and it was to be nothing less than the cradle of the post-war European avant-garde, for among its early members was the young Pierre Boulez.

Another pupil was the pianist Yvonne Loriod – 'a unique pianist, noble and of genius, whose existence transformed not only [my] writing for the piano but also [my] style, [my] view of the world and [my] way of thinking'[2] – for whom all Messiaen's later works for the instrument were to be written. The first of these, which they played together, was to inaugurate a period of great productivity during which Messiaen composed the following remarkable succession of works:

1943   *Visions de l'Amen* (two pianos) [seven movements]

1943–4 *Trois petites liturgies de la Présence Divine* (female chorus, piano, ondes Martenot, percussion and strings)

1944   *Vingt regards sur l'enfant Jésus* (piano)

1945   *Harawi* (voice and piano) [twelve songs]

1946   *Chant des déportés* (choir and large orchestra)

1946–8 *Turangalîla Symphony* (large orchestra with solo piano and *ondes Martenot*) [ten movements]

1948   *Cinq rechants* (mixed voices)

Messiaen was not to know then that Loriod would in due course become his second wife, for at this time his first wife Claire Delbos (the 'Mi' of *Poèmes pour Mi*), though sick, was still alive (she died in 1959). Amidst all his great work, Messiaen cared devotedly both for her and for their young son Pascal.[3]

Malcolm Hayes has suggested that the *Quatuor pour la fin du Temps* marked a turning point in Messiaen's career because the conditions of its production forced him to turn away from 'dependence on the essentially private inspiration of the early organ works and song cycles, and towards an unambiguous acceptance of the composer's public role'.[4] Certainly it is notable that Messiaen completed no organ works during the 1940s, whereas several of his most significant vocal pieces date from this period. Indeed, it was one of these that of all the music he composed at this time aroused the strongest critical feelings, when the first performance of the *Trois petites liturgies de la Présence Divine*, which took place under the baton of Roger Désormière in Paris on 21 April 1945, led to abusive attacks on Messiaen in the press. He was very much in the public eye at this time, as the *Vingt regards* were premiered only a matter of weeks before the *Trois petites liturgies*, and the *Quatuor* was also performed in Paris at this time.[5]

The composer later recalled the fuss that was made about the spoken commentaries with which he introduced each of the *Vingt regards* at their first performance:

> The story that surrounds these commentaries is completely idiotic. People wanted to see them as a surrealist manifesto, and they quoted from them dishonestly, lumping together bits that weren't meant to be next to each other. So that when the work was published, and they read these famous commentaries, my detractors were profoundly disappointed. I should add that I have a horror of speaking in public and of speaking of my works. I'd not spoken [of them] at all until my time of captivity. It was only after the necessity of introducing the *Quatuor pour la fin du Temps* to my fellow prisoners in the Stalag that I adopted the habit ... of analysing my music and that of others.[6]

Messiaen's adoption of this role as analyst came as his role as a performer was suddenly much reduced. Not only had he temporarily ceased to compose organ music, but he had a new interpreter for his piano music. Interpreting his compositions instead through the medium of spoken and written analytical commentary, Messiaen may be said to have provided a springboard for the young Boulez, who very quickly rose to prominence as a polemicist prepared to engage in a war of words about the values appropriate to new musical developments in the immediate post-war years.

Messiaen's official role at the Conservatoire as a professor of harmony, while his private classes were having such a significant impact on young composers, was perceived by some as an anomaly. Boulez in particular, who had studied in Messiaen's harmony class during the 1944–5 session,[7] was prominent in asking the Director of the Conservatoire, Claude Delvincourt, to create a composition class for Messiaen.[8] Yet Messiaen had aroused sufficient controversy for any change in his position at the Conservatoire to be a matter of extreme delicacy. An interesting summary of Messiaen's status in the Parisian musical scene at this time is to be found in a letter written to Igor Stravinsky by the publishing and broadcasting executive Roland Bourdariat in April 1945:

> Musicians here are divided into partisans for or against Messiaen and the chapel of ridiculous disciples that surrounds him, hypnotized by him, and in which, like Father Divine, he preaches a pseudo-mystical jargon. The religiosity of his sermons cannot hide an unbelievably vulgar sensuality, as well as false and absurd doctrines. These pupils hail the *Sacre* and *Noces* ... but create scandals at performances of every other work of yours.[9] Western music does not interest them, but only so-called Hindu rhythms and pseudo-Oriental melodies. ... For these Messiaenists, the greatest modern composer is Schoenberg.[10]

Despite the highly charged situation, in which both Boulez and the pro-Schoenberg commentator and teacher René Leibowitz played significant roles, Delvincourt was broadly supportive of Messiaen, and he found a happy way out of his dilemma by appointing Messiaen professor of analysis, æsthetics and rhythm in 1947. This was, in effect, an official recognition of the importance of Messiaen's private class, whose successor it became.[11] Messiaen's critics were disarmed, because student composers were not obliged to attend his classes, though they could elect to do so; at the same time Messiaen's freedom was maintained, because he was not obliged to teach composition:[12]

> I was addressing some very remarkable musicians, and I had to offer them whatever they hadn't learned in previous classes ... In composition classes, the correcting of students' work prevented professors from devoting much time to analyzing works of the masters and exotic, ancient, and ultramodern music: such analyses were the principal work of my class.[13]

It would be misleading to categorise any of Messiaen's own music as 'ultramodern', but a short piano piece he composed in 1949 was, despite its modest dimensions, a work of seminal importance to the far-reaching developments of post-Schoenbergian serial technique that were undertaken by Boulez and others in the early 1950s. This was 'Mode de valeurs et d'intensités', one of the *Quatre études de rythme* which, along with *Cantéyodjayâ* (also composed in 1949), displayed the new kind of pianism that Messiaen had created for Yvonne Loriod (though he himself also played these *études*). 'Mode de valeurs ...' was epoch-making in its extension of the concept of mode to embrace not only a collection of pitches but also a collection of durations, a collection of dynamic levels and a collection of pianistic articulations (*staccato*, *marcato*, etc.). Although these attributes were co-ordinated in Messiaen's piece – so that each note in the mode was fixed in pitch, dynamic, duration and articulation – it was a conceptually straightforward step (in hindsight at least) for Boulez to treat these elements separately using serial methods, as he did in his first book of *Structures* for two pianos, part of which he and Messiaen performed for the first time in Paris in 1952.

In view of the conscious separation of pitch, rhythm, tempo and register we have observed in the movements of the *Quatuor pour la fin du Temps*, it may seem surprising that Messiaen himself had not already chosen to do what Boulez would go on to attempt. But Messiaen's own approach to serial concepts, evidently deeply considered over the course of a decade or more, was not so much to extend as to undermine them. His technique of 'interversion' – which he used in 'Île de feu 2', another of the *Quatre études* – subverted the very concept of a single fixed ordering on which Schoenbergian serialism was based, by taking an existing sequence (12, 11, ... 1) and unfolding it outwards from the centre in alternate directions (6, 7, 5, 8, ... 1, 12) to make a new one. This was a mathematical transformation that could be cyclically repeated, like the rhythmic and harmonic pedals we have seen in the *Quatuor*,[14] and as such it anticipated approaches to composition that would be developed in the following decades by a number of composers in Europe and the United States. For Messiaen such things were a means rather than an end, however, as his inspiration remained firmly in nature and theology. Though proud of his technical achievements, he was not motivated by the development of new techniques either for their own sake or out of a perceived historical necessity to do so (in line with Adorno's analysis of the modernist composer's obligations).[15] In this sense, Messiaen's work already stood outside historical time – his battle for 'the end of time' had been fought and won.

Private echoes

More direct traces of the *Quatuor pour la fin du Temps* may be observed in a number of Messiaen's subsequent works. The *Turangalîla Symphony*, like the *Quatuor*, follows a multi-movement design encompassing a great variety of moods from the contemplative to the sturdily developmental. Its ten movements are carefully organised into interlocking cycles, taking further the distinction observed in the *Quatuor* between the contemplative framing movements (the first, fifth and eighth), the more overtly programmatic (second, third, sixth and seventh) and the uniquely interludial fourth movement. The interlocking cycles of *Turangalîla* may in turn have been a model for Boulez's *Le marteau sans maître* (1952–5).

The even larger multi-movement canvas of the *Vingt regards* has something of the same articulation, though this is as much a consequence of the treatment of musical themes as it is of the correspondences between types of movements that Messiaen identifies as follows:

> *Regards* referring to divinity recur every 5 numbers: nos. 1 [sic], 5, 10, 15 and 20. The 'Regard de la Croix' bears the number 7 (a perfect number) because the sufferings of Christ on the Cross restored the order that was disturbed by sin, and the Angels are confirmed in grace in no. 14 (two times 7). The 'Regard du Temps' bears the number 9 [representing] the nine months of maternity common to all children, and the 'Regard de l'Onction terrible' has the number 18 (two times 9) … The two pieces which speak of Creation and the Divine Government of Creation are no. 6 (because 6 is the number of [days of] creation) and no. 12 (two times 6).[16]

Although the correspondence of this plan with the design of the *Quatuor* is no more than a loose resemblance, it is notable that the tenth and twentieth *regards* include examples of the 'developmental' treatment of material which Messiaen had attempted in the crucial seventh movement of the *Quatuor*.

The major development in Messiaen's works of the 1950s was the so-called *stile oiseau*. Birdsongs had appeared in the *Quatuor* and other works of the 1940s as characteristic elements, but they did not dominate the musical invention. Now, in works such as *Reveil des oiseaux*

(1953, piano and orchestra), *Oiseaux exotiques* (1955–6, piano with wind and percussion ensemble), and above all in the vast solo piano cycle *Catalogue d'oiseaux*, birdsong carried the musical and programmatic focus. Although this style seemed essentially new, and could perhaps be seen as a retreat into a world of private communion after the public tribulations of the 1940s and the ascent of Boulez as the standard-bearer among French composers, direct connections with the *Quatuor* may nonetheless be observed.

Most remarkable, perhaps, is the uncanny similarity in tone between Messiaen's description of his capture by German soldiers, as related to Antoine Goléa at around the time the *Catalogue* was being composed, and the composer's introductory paragraphs to some movements of the piano cycle. Compare this account – almost musical in itself – of how Messiaen and his companions were taken prisoner in a forest near Nancy:

> we were taken prisoner in a forest, by means of choirs of speaking voices [*des chœurs parlés*] … The Germans posted themselves at the four points of the compass, in small numbers, and scanned rhythmically certain words. The different sources of the sounds of these words multiplied, giving the illusion of a large troop. The chorus closed in a small circle on the [four] Frenchmen, who believed themselves outnumbered.[17]

with the composer's prefatory remarks to 'L'alouette Lulu':

> From the col of the *grand bois* at St-Saveur en Rue, in the mountains of the Forez. Pinewoods to the right of the road, fields to the left. High in the sky, in the darkness, the Woodlark peel away two by two: a chromatic, fluid descent. Hidden in a thicket, in a clearing in the wood, a Nightingale responds, its biting tremolos set in contrast with the mysterious voice from on high. A Woodlark, invisible, draws near, fades. The trees and fields are dark and still. It is midnight.[18]

In the music of the individual movements of the *Catalogue*, Messiaen portrays not only the birds but also their habitats, interpreting both alike as manifestations of the Divine in nature. A number of the movements follow the opening of the *Quatuor* in juxtaposing the mechanical, 'timeless' music of intangible natural forces against the fluidity of carefully transcribed birdsong: among these, 'Le chocard des alpes', which presents the song of the alpine chough against a back-drop of glaciers, is a particularly striking example. What is missing, though, is the intensity of the theological inspiration that makes the *Quatuor* so remarkable.

Messiaen scarcely returned to chamber music at all in the fifty years that followed the *Quatuor*. Writing for small ensemble had been forced on him by peculiar circumstances and he seems not to have found it amenable. Towards the end of his life, however, he came close to completing a *Concert à quatre*, scored for orchestra with a quartet of soloists: flute, oboe, cello and piano.[19] If this correspondence is coincidental, there is a more valid comparison to be made between the *Quatuor* and the composer's last great orchestral canvas, *Éclairs sur l'au-delà …* (1987–91), which – as suggested by its title ('Illuminations of the Beyond …') – is concerned explicitly with the afterlife. The inscriptions to six of its eleven movements are taken in whole or in part from the book of Revelation, and the sixth (and central) movement in particular, 'Les sept Anges aux sept trompettes', revisits the theological subject matter of the *Quatuor*. The music is very different in sound, being dominated by forceful brass and percussion, but the unison melody links it with the sixth movement of the *Quatuor*, the similarly entitled 'Danse de la fureur, pour les sept trompettes'. In addition, both the fifth movement of *Éclairs* and the last are threnodies very much in the same vein as the fifth and the last movements of the *Quatuor*. In each work, the three movements stand similarly in relation to the organisation of the entire sequence.

The *Quatuor pour la fin du Temps* is by no means set apart, then, from Messiaen's other works; indeed in some ways it was crucial to his development as an artist. It is not the only musical work to derive its great power of utterance from having been composed in captivity during the Second World War, nor is it the only musical work of consequence to be based on the events of the apocalypse, as the example of Franz Schmidt's oratorio *Das Buch mit sieben Siegeln* (1938) serves to demonstrate. But it remains a unique document of a great composer at the height of his powers responding to extraordinary circumstances with sustained and magnificent invention.

Appendix

Messiaen's modes à transpositions limitées

In the preface to *La Nativité du Seigneur*, and later in *Technique*, Messiaen describes and tabulates seven 'modes of limited transposition'. These are pitch-class collections with properties of internal organisation that restrict the number of distinct transpositional levels of each collection to significantly fewer than the twelve that are available to most other collections, including the diatonic major scale.

Each collection is itself generated by successive transpositions of a small cell of a few notes, giving a characteristic repertoire of melodic configurations, and each with the exception of modes 1 and 5 also contains a number of triads and/or other harmonies familiar from tonal music, something which Messiaen was able to exploit musically. The regular internal structure of the modes means that where one such harmony is found, others will be found at regular intervals from it, allowing the composer '[either] to give predominance to one of the tonalities or to leave the tonal impression unsettled'.[1] For example, the form of mode 2 which contains the C major triad also includes the E♭ major, F♯ major and A major triads. The tonal focus might settle for a while on any one of these, or they might be cycled in quick succession.

Mode 1

This mode, known elsewhere as the whole-tone scale, is entirely regular in construction, being generated by the six-fold transposition of a single note at successive intervals of two semitones (ic2). The collection thus exists at two levels of transposition, which are here distinguished as t0 and t1. In these labels, 't' is an abbreviation for 'transposition', and the number after it indicates the upward interval

96

(measured in semitones) through which each is transposed, relative to what Messiaen calls the 'first' transposition:[2]

Feeling that this collection had already been widely exposed in the music of his predecessors, including Debussy and Dukas, Messiaen says that he prefers to deploy it where it could be 'concealed in a superposition of modes which renders it unrecognizable'.[3]

Mode 2

This mode is known in the Stravinsky literature as the octatonic scale,[4] and is generated from a two-note cell transposed successively at ic3:

Mode 2 is a rich resource of triads and other recognised harmonies, since each transposition includes four major triads, to which the familiar minor sevenths and minor ninths can be added. Messiaen also associates mode 2 with the chord of the added (major) sixth, and with a sonority comprising a major triad with added augmented fourth.

Mode 3

This mode may be seen as an extension of the 'hexatonic' collection which has been shown to underpin some of the expansions of tonality undertaken by composers such as Liszt, Wagner and Brahms,[5] though there is no evidence that Messiaen was explicitly aware of the connection. It is generated by successive transpositions at ic4 of a three-note cell (e.g. D–E♭–E♮ in the t0 form of the mode):

Each transposition of mode 3 contains six each of major and minor triads, together with major seventh chords, dominant sevenths, half-diminished sevenths, minor triads with major seventh, and augmented triads. Note also that each transposition of mode 3 contains a complete whole-tone collection (mode 1). In addition, this mode is closely associated with Messiaen's 'chord of resonance':

This sonority is derived from the acoustic overtones of the root, here C♮ (see p. 33). The chord shown above contains eight of the nine pcs of the t0 form of mode 3.

Modes 4–7

These modes are used less frequently than modes 2 and 3, perhaps because they are less individually distinctive. Mode 5 is a truncated form of both modes 4 and 6, which are in turn truncated forms of mode 7. Each exists at six transpositional levels, of which Messiaen's 'first' transposition is shown below for each mode:

Note that mode 7 excludes only two pcs of the twelve available. Each of its transpositions includes a version not only of modes 4 and 6 but also of mode 2. Each transposition of mode 6 also includes a version of mode 1.

Notes

Introduction

1 Messiaen's account of his capture is discussed on p. 94.

2 Goléa, *Rencontres*, p. 60; Pasquier, 'Hommage', p. 91.

3 Goléa, *Rencontres*, p. 61.

4 See, for example, Griffiths, *Olivier Messiaen*, pp. 24–7.

5 See Messiaen, '*Ariane et Barbe-bleue* de Paul Dukas', *La revue musicale*, 166 (1936), pp. 79–86.

6 Samuel, *Olivier Messiaen: Music and Color*, pp. 110–11.

7 *Ibid.*, p. 112.

8 *Ibid.*, pp. 112–13.

9 *Ibid.*, pp. 72–3.

10 Samuel, *Conversations*, p. 40. (A different translation is to be found in Samuel, *Olivier Messiaen: Music and Color*, p. 73.)

11 Messiaen, 'Préface', p. ii.

12 Messiaen: 'the notions of "metre" and "tempo" are replaced by the feeling of a short value (the semiquaver, for example) and its multiples' (*ibid.*, p. ii).

13 The names of this writer and his treatise have been transliterated in many different ways for readers of the English and French languages. The transliterations used here follow those used in Samuel, *Olivier Messiaen: Music and Color*.

14 See, for example, Wasantha W. Singh, *Musical India: An Advanced Treatise on the History, Theory, and Practice of India's Music* (New York: Pageant-Poseidon, 1975), pp. 7–13 ('Sangita').

15 Messiaen, 'Préface', pp. iii–iv.

16 Samuel, *Olivier Messiaen: Music and Color*, p. 74, cf. Messiaen, *Technique*, Vol. 2, Ex. 30.

17 Samuel, *Olivier Messiaen: Music and Color*, p. 75; cf. Messiaen, *Technique*, Vol. 1, p. 14.

18 See Messiaen, 'Le rythme chez Igor Stravinsky', *La revue musicale*, 191 (1939), pp. 91–2.

19 Samuel, *Olivier Messiaen: Music and Color*, pp. 112–13.

5 The pcs all lie within mode 3, in the same transposition as is employed at *ii*/C:1ff. and H:1ff.
6 cf. Messiaen, *Technique*, Vol. 2, Exs. 114–15.
7 Messiaen, *Technique*, Vol. 1, p. 51.
8 Messiaen, *Conférence de Notre-Dame*, pp. 8–9.
9 The corresponding example in *Technique* (Vol. 2, Ex. 208) spells the A♭ as G♯.
10 The notional effect of inversion is perhaps not unlike the relationship between acoustic resonance and 'inferior resonance'.
11 Messiaen, *Traité*, Vol. 1, p. 66. I am grateful to Christopher Dingle for drawing this to my attention.
12 Messiaen, *Conférence de Notre-Dame*, p. 8.
13 Messiaen makes this connection explicitly, but does not claim scientific support (*ibid.*, pp. 8–9; also Samuel, *Olivier Messiaen: Music and Color*, pp. 61–2).
14 Leonid Sabaneev [Sabanejew], 'Prometheus von Skrjabin', in *Der blaue Reiter*, ed. W. Kandinsky and F. Marc, new edn (Munich: Piper, 1965; orig. publ. 1912), pp. 107–24 (pp. 113–16).
15 This substitution arguably renders Scriabin's collection closer to the acoustical facts than is Messiaen's.
16 Kenneth Peacock, 'Synæsthetic Perception: Alexander Scriabin's Color Hearing', *Music Perception*, 2/iv (1985), pp. 483–505 (pp. 493–4).
17 Samuel, *Conversations*, p. 16.
18 Samuel, *Olivier Messiaen: Music and Color*, p. 64.
19 Bernard, 'Messiaen's Synæsthesia', p. 47; 'Colour', p. 207.
20 Bernard, 'Messiaen's Synæsthesia', pp. 57–60; 'Colour', pp. 210–11.
21 Messiaen, *Technique*, Vol. 1, pp. 51–3 (the quoted passage appears on p. 52).
22 Griffiths, *Olivier Messiaen*, pp. 203–4.
23 Messiaen, *Conférence de Notre-Dame*, p. 9; Samuel, *Olivier Messiaen: Music and Color*, p. 61.
24 Samuel, *Olivier Messiaen: Music and Color*, pp. 64–5.
25 Messiaen, 'Olivier Messiaen analyse ses œuvres', in *Hommage à Olivier Messiaen: novembre–décembre 1978* (Paris: La recherche artistique, 1979), cited in Bernard, 'Messiaen's Synæsthesia', pp. 57 and 68.

3 'Abîme des oiseaux'

1 Messiaen, 'Préface', p. i.
2 Matheson, 'The End of Time', p. 235.
3 Bar locations in this movement – which being written for one instrument has no rehearsal letters in Messiaen's score – are identified in this book with reference to the letter-names used in the table on p. 41.

4 Messiaen, *Technique*, Vol. 1, pp. 31–3; Vol. 2, Exs. 75–113.
5 Messiaen's melody is given first rather than second in Example 3.1, since Ex. 3.1b is derived from it; the discussion takes them in reverse order in order to emphasise Messiaen's invention.
6 Messiaen, *Technique*, Vol. 2, Ex. 77.
7 Messiaen, 'Préface', p. ii.
8 *Ibid.*, p. iii.
9 Goléa, *Rencontres*, p. 65.
10 Messiaen, *Technique*, Vol. 2, Ex. 114.
11 If the composition of this movement was begun in a field near Nancy, as Pasquier later recalled ('Hommage', p. 91; see p. 8), then the birdsongs could conceivably have been notated there.
12 Messiaen, *Technique*, Vol. 2, Exs. 114–15.
13 cf. the highly dramatic use of a similar manipulation of registers towards the end of the sixth movement (see pp. 70–71).

4 'Intermède'

1 Messiaen, 'Préface', p. i.
2 Goléa, *Rencontres*, p. 65.
3 Messiaen, *Technique*, Vol. 1, pp. 28–9.
4 *Ibid.*, p. 28.
5 *Ibid.*, p. 29 (translation slightly adapted).
6 cf. Messiaen, *Technique*, Vol. 2, Exs. 68–9.

5 'Louange à l'Éternité de Jésus'

1 Messiaen, 'Préface', p. ii.
2 Griffiths, *Olivier Messiaen*, p. 105.
3 Messiaen, essay accompanying STU 70102 (the biblical reference is to John 4:14).
4 The score of *Fête des belles eaux* is held in private hands and could not be consulted during the writing of this book. I should like to thank the staff of the National Sound Archive (British Library) for giving me the opportunity to study the work from a recording.
5 Messiaen may have been reminded of this spectacle on seeing the aurora borealis while in the prison camp (see n. 44 to the Introduction).
6 Messiaen, *Technique*, Vol. 1, p. 37.
7 Messiaen, *Technique*, Vol. 2, Exs. 129–31, and accompanying descriptions (Vol. 1, p. 37).

8 Messiaen shows only where the second of these internal periods begins; the location of the third is interpreted here.

9 Messiaen, *Technique*, Vol. 1, p. 38.

10 Messiaen, *Technique*, Vol. 1, pp. 58, 64.

11 Some notes of these triads are spelled enharmonically in the notations of the modes given in the Appendix.

12 Joel Lester, *Analytic Approaches to Twentieth-Century Music* (New York: Norton, 1989), pp. 165–6.

13 In *Fête des belles eaux*, the three parts are of course taken by separate monophonic instruments.

14 Messiaen, *Technique*, Vol. 1, p. 37.

15 In particular, the role of the total-chromatic collection merits close consideration, as does the association of recurrent melodic formulæ with particular forms of multi-collection interaction. Above all it would be appropriate to investigate how multi-collection interactions relate to concepts of structural levels.

16 This description equates 'modulation' with a change of referential collection, which happens also to be the sense in with Messiaen uses the term 'modulation' in *Technique*, Vol. 1, pp. 65–6, under the headings 'Modulation of a mode to itself' and 'Modulation of a mode to another mode'.

6 'Danse de la fureur, pour les sept trompettes'

1 Messiaen, 'Préface', p. ii.

2 It is perhaps tempting to hear the climactic restatement of the theme at *vi*/O:1ff. as the seventh and last trump. But the Angel of Revelation 10 actually appears after the sixth trumpet and its ensuing catastrophes, to remind the world of the awesome consequences of the seventh.

3 cf. Messiaen, *Technique*, Vol. 2, Ex. 13.

4 This is the view put forward by Joel Lester in *Analytic Approaches to Twentieth-Century Music* (New York: Norton, 1989), p. 159.

5 Messiaen, *Technique*, Vol. 1, p. 59. See also p. 20.

6 Messiaen, *Technique*, Vol. 1, p. 33; Vol. 2, Ex. 113.

7 EMI CZS 7 67400 2 (EMI France, 1992; recorded 1956).

8 See Messiaen, 'Préface', p. iii.

9 Messiaen, *Technique*, Vol. 1, p. 36.

10 Messiaen's own recorded performance of this movement (Musidisc RC 719) is fascinating in its use of unmarked tempo changes to articulate the progress of the music, very much in line with his advice to performers that 'they should not be afraid of the exaggerated nuances – the accel-

erandos, rallentandos, all that makes an interpretation lively and sensitive' ('Préface', p. iv). The opening of the theme is played by Messiaen and his ensemble with a certain deliberation on each occurrence, whereas its concluding phrase has a slight urgency to it and the passages in constant semiquavers tend always to press forward (the marking 'pressez un peu' in *vi*/E:6 is considerably anticipated, for example).

7 'Fouillis d'arcs-en-ciel, pour l'Ange qui annonce la fin du Temps'

1 Messiaen, 'Préface', p. ii. In the version of this text in Goléa, *Rencontres*, pp. 72–3, the second sentence is cast in the third person: 'In his dreams, the author hears recognised chords and melodies, he sees known colours and forms ... he passes beyond reality and submits in ecstasy ...'
2 Messiaen, *Technique*, Vol. 1, pp. 42–3.
3 There is an intriguing discrepancy between the score of the *Quatuor*, in which the piano part is marked *p* at *vii*/A:1, and the schematic representation of this passage in Ex. 359 of Messiaen's *Technique* (Vol. 2), where the piano part is marked *mf*.
4 Messiaen, *Technique*, Vol. 1, p. 42.
5 See Carl Dahlhaus, 'What is "Developing Variation"?', in *Schoenberg and the New Music: Essays by Carl Dahlhaus*, trans. Derrick Puffett and Alfred Clayton (Cambridge: Cambridge University Press, 1987), pp. 128–33.
6 Note that the rhythm of the violin and cello parts in Ex. 7.2a is non-retrogradable (1 1 1 1 1 2 2 1 1 1 1 1 semiquavers). I am grateful to Sarah Pickering for drawing this to my attention.
7 Arnold Schoenberg, *Fundamentals of Musical Composition*, ed. Gerald Strang and Leonard Stein (London: Faber, 1967), pp. 58, 153.
8 Goléa, *Rencontres*, p. 65.
9 cf. Messiaen, *Technique*, Vol. 2, Ex. 168.
10 cf. *ibid.*, Ex. 99.
11 Goléa, *Rencontres*, p. 66.
12 See Edward T. Cone, 'Stravinsky: The Progress of a Method', in *Perspectives on Schoenberg and Stravinsky*, ed. Benjamin Boretz and Edward T. Cone (New York: Norton, 1972), pp. 155–64.
13 Messiaen, *Technique*, Vol. 1, p. 14.
14 *Ibid.*, p. 43.
15 Messiaen, *Technique*, Vol. 2, Ex. 250.
16 See note 1.
17 Messiaen, 'Préface', p. i.

18 cf. Messiaen, *Technique*, Vol. 1, p. 43.
19 cf. Messiaen, *Technique*, Vol. 2, Ex. 169.
20 Messiaen, *Technique*, Vol. 1, p. 21 (the passage is repeated on p. 63).

8 'Louange à l'Immortalité de Jésus'

1 Messiaen, 'Préface', p. ii.
2 See Griffiths, *Olivier Messiaen*, pp. 95–6.
3 EMI CZS 7 67400 2. The durations given here for the scores are calculated using Messiaen's metronome markings, without allowance for the 'un peu ralenti' in bar *viii*/D:6 of the *Quatuor*, or for the fermata in the last bar of both movements or for the rubato that is liable to occur in performance. The final minim rest in the *Quatuor* is omitted from the calculation.
4 In Messiaen's recording of the *Quatuor* (Musidisc RC 719) the movement has a duration of approx. 7′20″, but since the performance is notable for its quickening of the slow tempos and overplaying of the quiet dynamics this duration is probably misleading. A better indication of Messiaen's preferred tempo is perhaps to be gleaned from the commercial recording of the *Quatuor* with Yvonne Loriod as pianist (EMI CD C 7 54395 2), in which this movement lasts 8′28″.
5 Messiaen, *Technique*, Vol. 1, p. 38.
6 cf. the analytical discussion of the seventh of Messiaen's Preludes in Pople, 'Messiaen's Musical Language', pp. 26–9.
7 Messiaen, *Technique*, Vol. 1, p. 38.
8 *Ibid.*, p. 53.
9 *Ibid.*, p. 38.

9 Contexts

1 Samuel, *Olivier Messiaen: Music and Color*, p. 177.
2 Goléa, *Rencontres*, p. 147. Messiaen writes of himself here in the third person.
3 See 'Interview with Yvonne Loriod', in *The Messiaen Companion*, ed. Peter Hill (London: Faber, 1995), pp. 283–303 (p. 294).
4 Malcolm Hayes, 'Instrumental, Orchestral and Choral Works to 1948', in *The Messiaen Companion*, ed. Peter Hill (London: Faber, 1995), pp. 157–200 (pp. 180–81).
5 It is worth recalling that as these premieres took place the war in Europe,

though approaching its conclusion, was not yet over. Paris had been liberated towards the end of August 1944, but the German surrender was yet to come, on 7 May 1945.

6 Goléa, *Rencontres*, pp. 103–4.

7 Peter Heyworth, 'The First Fifty Years', in *Pierre Boulez: A Symposium*, ed. William Glock (London: Eulenburg, 1986), pp. 3–39 (p. 9).

8 Goléa, *Rencontres*, p. 239.

9 Bourdariat probably refers to the protest led by Boulez at the first Paris performance of Stravinsky's *Dances concertantes* on 23 February 1945.

10 Letter of 25 April 1945 from Roland Bourdariat to Igor Stravinsky, trans. in *Stravinsky: Selected Correspondence*, ed. Robert Craft, Vol. 2 (New York: Knopf, 1984), pp. 515–16.

11 Samuel, *Olivier Messiaen: Music and Color*, p. 177.

12 Goléa, *Rencontres*, pp. 240–41.

13 Samuel, *Olivier Messiaen: Music and Color*, p. 176.

14 After nine further transformations of this kind, the original sequence is regained.

15 Theodor W. Adorno, *Philosophy of Modern Music*, trans. Anne G. Mitchell and Wesley V. Blomster (New York: Seabury, 1973).

16 Messiaen, preface to *Vingt regards sur l'enfant Jésus*.

17 Goléa, *Rencontres*, pp. 59–60.

18 Messiaen, preface to *Catalogue d'oiseaux*, book 3.

19 The orchestration of the concerto was completed by Yvonne Loriod with advice from Heinz Holliger and George Benjamin, and the work was first performed in 1994.

Appendix

1 Messiaen, *Technique*, Vol. 1, pp. 58, 64.

2 Messiaen's referential forms of the modes do not in every case correspond to the 'normal' forms of the related pitch-class collections defined in the standard work on the subject, Allen Forte's *The Structure of Atonal Music* (New Haven: Yale University Press, 1973). Forte's labels (set-class names) for Messiaen's modal collections are as follows: 6–35, 8–28, 9–12, 8–9, 6–7, 8–25 and 10–6; his 'normal' forms correspond respectively to the t0, t0, t2, t1, t1, t2 and t1 forms of the modes as labelled here. The discrepancy can be ascribed to a contrast between Forte's desire for mathematical consistency and Messiaen's feeling for pitch centricity, which is expressed in the composer's choice of starting pitches in his notation of the modes.

3 Messiaen, *Technique*, Vol. 1, p. 59.

4 See Arthur Berger, 'Problems of Pitch Organization in Stravinsky', in *Perspectives on Schoenberg and Stravinsky*, ed. Benjamin Boretz and Edward T. Cone (New York: Norton, 1972), pp. 123–54; Pieter C. van den Toorn, *The Music of Igor Stravinsky* (New Haven: Yale University Press, 1983).

5 Richard Cohn, 'Maximally Smooth Cycles, Hexatonic Systems, and the Analysis of Late-Romantic Triadic Progressions', *Music Analysis*, 15/i (1995), pp. 9–40.

Select bibliography

Bernard, Jonathan W., 'Messiaen's Synæsthesia: The Correspondence between Color and Sound Structure in his Music', *Music Perception*, 4 (1986), pp. 41–68

'Colour', in *The Messiaen Companion*, ed. Peter Hill (London: Faber, 1995), pp. 203–19

Goléa, Antoine, *Rencontres avec Olivier Messiaen* (Paris: Juillard, 1960)

Griffiths, Paul, *Olivier Messiaen and the Music of Time* (London: Faber, 1985)

Matheson, Iain G., 'The End of Time: A Biblical Theme in Messiaen's *Quatuor*', in *The Messiaen Companion*, ed. Peter Hill (London: Faber, 1995), pp. 234–48

Messiaen, Olivier, 'Préface' to miniature score of *Quatuor pour la fin du temps* (Paris: Durand, 1942), pp. i–iv

Technique de mon langage musical, 2 vols. (Paris: Leduc, 1944). Vol. 1, trans. J. Satterfield, published as *The Technique of my Musical Language* (Paris: Leduc, 1956)

Conférence de Bruxelles [prononcé à l'Exposition Internationale de Bruxelles en 1958] (Paris: Leduc, 1960)

Conférence de Notre-Dame [prononcé à Notre-Dame de Paris le 4 décembre 1977] (Paris: Leduc, 1978)

Traité de rythme, de couleur, et d'ornithologie, 5 vols. (Paris: Leduc, 1994–)

Pasquier, Étienne, 'Hommage à Olivier Messiaen', in programme book to the cycle of Messiaen's organ works at La Trinité, Paris (1995), pp. 91–2

Pople, Anthony, 'Messiaen's Musical Language: An Introduction', in *The Messiaen Companion*, ed. Peter Hill (London: Faber, 1995), pp. 15–50

Samuel, Claude, *Conversations with Olivier Messiaen*, trans. Felix Aprahamian (London: Stainer and Bell, 1976)

Olivier Messiaen: Music and Color [conversations with Claude Samuel], trans. E. Thomas Glasow (Portland, OR: Amadeus Press, 1994)

Sherlaw Johnson, Robert, *Messiaen*, 2nd edn (London: Dent, 1989)

Index

Index